Healthy Preschoolers

• At School   • At Home

Healthy Preschoolers

- **At School**   - **At Home**

A fun-filled sourcebook to help
families reinforce what their
children are learning about health in
preschool, *plus* annotated lists of
books and resources.

Alice R. McCarthy, Ph.D.

Illustrations by Richard Eric Wilson

BRIDGE
COMMUNICATIONS, INC.

Healthy Preschoolers: At School and At Home was written in part from a grant from the Michigan Department of Education, Lansing, Michigan, to the Monroe County Intermediate School District, Monroe, Michigan. Several of the family resource chapters were written with the assistance of the Drug-Free Youth and Families Initiative Grant to the Wayne County Regional Education Service Agency, Wayne, Michigan. This grant was received from the Skillman Foundation, Detroit, Michigan. Bridge Communications, Inc. gratefully acknowledges permission to publish these writings.

Library of Congress Catalog Card Number 94-72479.

ISBN 9621645-2-6

Printed in the United States of America.
First Printing: October 1994; Second Printing: March 1995

94 95 96 97 ◆ 10 9 8 76 5 4 3 2 1

Joe Crachiola, Cover Photograph
Marcy Johnson, Administrative Assistant to the President, Bridge Communications, Inc.
Jim McCarthy, Executive Editor
Kay Spors, Computer Answer, Inc., Design and Production
Richard Eric Wilson, Illustrations

Includes bibliographical references.

Books from Bridge Communications, Inc. are available at quantity discounts with bulk purchase (500 and over) for educational use. Contact: Bridge Communications, Inc., (810) 646-1020; (810) 646-5583; FAX (810) 644-8546.

Foreword

Early education is a critical first step on a life-long path of learning. Development and learning occur as young children interact with their families and teachers. Adults—especially adults in families and teachers in preschool—promote learning and development by creating a healthy setting. A healthy setting provides space, materials, and the opportunity for play. In this setting, adults encourage, nurture, stimulate, and talk with young children. In some educational settings a healthy environment includes an emphasis on health issues and teaching specific health lessons.

Healthy Preschoolers is published to encourage teaching health principles to preschoolers both at school and at home. The booklet is based on the philosophy that families are the young child's most important teachers and that families want a deep and continued involvement in their child's schooling.

Healthy Preschoolers demonstrates how families and schools can work together to set the stage for healthy lifestyles even while children are very young. The booklet is probably the first to describe what children are learning about health in preschool and to encourage families to build on these health lessons.

This booklet is a primer for families and teachers of young children on the important issues of health—nutrition, safety, sexual abuse, immunization, violence, conflict resolution, disease prevention, and mental health. The booklet also includes additional resources for parents and teachers about how children grow and how families can help prepare their children to eventually become strong, active readers. The serious issues facing families as they work to foster good health in their children are treated with openness, awareness, and hope.

The sixteen chapters in **Healthy Preschoolers** are easy to follow. Each chapter is divided into brief descriptions of health teachings at school and how the family can add to the health lessons taught. The *Getting it Straight* and *Another Look* sections found in each chapter, provide new health information for families and prompt families to use what they have read.

The extensive listings of books, pamphlets, organizations, and places to call encourage families, teachers, and administrators to seek additional help and information. The author worked especially hard to make this section a genuine resource for those wishing additional reading and/or assistance.

Dr. Alice R. McCarthy is uniquely qualified to address the important concerns raised in **Healthy Preschoolers**. She was first trained in childhood education at Cornell University. Her long experience working with schools began as the mother of five children, and her recent graduate work in curriculum development and the family adds to a deep understanding and empathy toward families and toward schools. Dr. McCarthy understands the cumulative impact of research findings that show the importance of the family in contributing to the progress of children in school, as well as the day-to-day challenges faced by families and by schools.

Dr. McCarthy appreciates the role of the school in teaching health principles to preschoolers. **Healthy Preschoolers** is designed to show schools that health and learning are dependent upon each other. Finally, **Healthy Preschoolers** shows families and schools how to make a real difference in the lives and health of young children. **Healthy Preschoolers** is a commendable piece of work.

Patricia Nichols, B.S.N., M.S.
Supervisor, Comprehensive Programs in Health and Early Childhood
Michigan Department of Education

Acknowledgments

This book is for the families of preschoolers. *Healthy Preschoolers* was created from a series of parent resource materials developed to accompany a health education curriculum written by Kit Payne, Ph.D. Dr. Payne is a member of the faculty in the College of Human Ecology, Michigan State University. She is also on the faculty at Central Michigan University and is an educational consultant.

Terri Langton, M.Ed., M. Pub. Admin., health educator, Monroe County Intermediate School District, Monroe, Michigan, initially asked that these *Good For You!* materials be written, included in the curriculum, and sent home to families. Ten chapters of *Healthy Preschoolers* were written with the aid of a grant to the Monroe Intermediate School District from the Michigan Department of Education. An additional six chapters were written as part of the Skillman Drug-Free Youth and Families Initiative grant to the Wayne County Regional Education Service Agency (WCRESA), Wayne, Michigan, from the Skillman Foundation in Detroit. The grant was coordinated by Adrea Kenyon Unitis, M.P.H., health educator, who along with Ms. Langton believed that families would enjoy knowing what their children were studying about health in school. All of these efforts were driven by a belief, that families are important in reinforcing health lessons taught at school. The author wishes to express her sincere appreciation to Ms. Langton and Ms. Unitis for their support.

The author also wishes to acknowledge Kit Payne, Ph.D., and Barbara Papania, Ed.D., Consultant, Preschool Education, Wayne County RESA, for their comprehensive editorial review. Their assistance and encouragement has made *Healthy Preschoolers* more helpful, complete, and most important, more useful to parents. Marcia Girson, M.A., health educator assisted with portions of the writing.

Craig Spangler, D.D.S., reviewed the dental health chapter. Randall S. Pope, Chief HIV/AIDS Prevention and Intervention Section, Michigan Department of Public Health, and Joy Schumacher, R.N., B.S.N., Oakland County Department of Public Health, Michigan, made numerous helpful suggestions related to the HIV/AIDS material. Ruth Ann Dunn, M.D., Chief, Immunization Section, Michigan Department of Public Health, reviewed the immunization section.

Reviewers from Children's Hospital of Michigan gave freely of their expertise. Nancy Delany, Coordinator, Child Passenger Safety Program and Pat Vranesich, R.N., nurse educator, made many suggestions for the safe kids chapter. Kurt Weiss, Occupant Protection Coordinator, Michigan Office of Highway Safety Planning also helped with this chapter.

Susan Smolinske, Pharm.D., Managing Director of the Poison Control Center at Children's Hospital of Michigan and John Trestrail, Director, Blodgett Regional Poison Control Center, Grand Rapids assisted with the chapter on poisons.

Special thanks also to Richard Eric Wilson for the delightful illustrations conceptualized and prepared especially for this publication.

Still further thanks need to go to Marcy Johnson, my assistant, and to Kay Spors. I owe a tremendous debt to both Marcy and Kay for their patience and understanding during the preparation of the manuscript and their continual willingness to re-input and re-format new material.

Alice R. McCarthy, Ph.D.

Healthy Preschoolers

A look inside this book

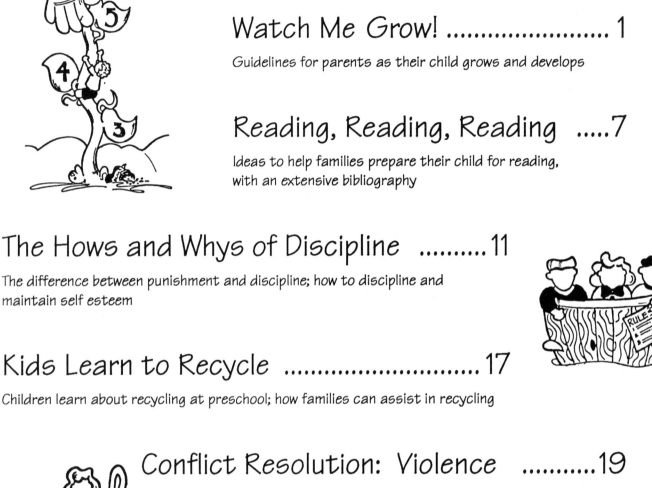

This book is dedicated to the caretakers of young children

—their families, and their teachers—

and to the good health of preschoolers.

Good for You!

Watch Me Grow!

At School:

Different ways to grow

Starting preschool is an important step in the development of a young child. Your child will be going through a lot of changes. For many youngsters, going to preschool is their first experience being away from home for any length of time. Preschool can be a difficult period of adjustment for some children. Children need patience and understanding as they try to become more independent.

In preschool health classes, children learn about different ways that people grow and develop. Children learn how to help their bodies grow by eating healthy foods, exercising, and getting enough rest. They learn new skills that help their minds grow, as well as social skills that will help them grow emotionally.

The preschool years are a time when children learn largely through play. They learn about their environment by climbing and exploring.

At School: (continued)

Children develop muscle coordination by coloring, painting, cutting, as well as running and playing games. Children also grow up in language development at a rapid pace.

Another very important skill that children learn in preschool is how to cooperate and how to get along with others. Preschool health lessons help children learn about sharing, cooperating with others, and talking about their feelings. These lessons help children get along with people in the larger society as well as within the family. As children learn to interact with others, they gain confidence, self esteem, and independence.

Your preschooler is learning in leaps and bounds. Enjoy this period of growth in your child. Don't be surprised at your child's new skills.

At Home:

How should my child be growing and developing?

Children grow and develop at different rates. Each child is unique and develops according to his or her own timetable. There is a wide range of normal development. Some children may learn language skills quickly and lag behind in their physical development; other children may be just the opposite. Don't compare your child's development with other children. Most children eventually learn the skills that are appropriate for their age level, although

they may learn at different rates. See *Getting It Straight* for a brief summary of growth and development in three-, four-, and five-year-olds.

What can I do to help my child?

All parents want to help their children to grow and reach their full potential. Here are some tips on child development from experts Dr. T. Berry Brazelton of Harvard Medical School, and Eli Saltz, Ph.D., director of the Merrill Palmer Institute, Wayne State University:

- **The most important developmental need of young children is a sense of emotional security.** Most of all, kids need to know that their parents are always there for them, no matter what. Emotional security is essential to building the self esteem and confidence needed later in life.

- **Your child needs free time to daydream, play, and rest.** Don't push your child to do more than he or she is capable of doing, either physically or mentally.

- **You may need to repeat requests for behavior change several times,** or in different ways before your child understands what you want. Your child will become self-directed if he or she receives consistent, clear directions from you.

2

At Home: (continued)

- **Understand your child's growth and development.** Your child is still developing the ability to distinguish real from make-believe. This is why it is common for young children to exaggerate the truth in ways that adults sometimes understand as telling lies. Your child's sense of judgment is still developing. Your patient guidance is needed to help your child decide what is right and what is wrong.

- **Enjoy your children.** The best thing you can do for your child is to let them know that you enjoy being with them. Given the time and attention he or she needs, a child will develop a sense of security and self confidence.

Have fun learning with your child.

Learning should always be fun. Don't push too hard. Try some of the fun activities below to help your child learn:

- **Read together.** Young children love books. Make a friend of your child's librarian and ask for his or her help in choosing books. Be prepared to read some books over and over; children quickly choose favorites. Children identify with the pictures on the page and the characters in the stories. Expand on the stories and listen to what your child says.

- **Include your children in the work schedule of your family.** Helping your child make a contribution to the smooth running of the household is a highly effective way to boost your child's self esteem.

- **Provide interesting opportunities for play.** Kids don't need expensive toys to have fun. Kids love to dress up. Old clothes, packing boxes, and material for making tents can provide hours of imaginative play.

- **Take your kids on field trips to the zoo, parks and playgrounds.**

- **Involve your children in the day-to-day life of the family.** Talk to your child about what's going on in the family and listen carefully to their comments. Such conversations give you a chance to clarify what your child is thinking.

- **Encourage your child to try new things.** You don't always need to plan specific activities, or even learning games. Children can learn a great deal through everyday interactions. Involve children in your hobbies and your work. Be sure your child knows where you work. If it is safe and appropriate, bring your child for a visit to your workplace. Even a Saturday visit works well.

Getting It Straight:

Children grow and develop at different rates. However, there are normal signs of growth and development. The following guidelines have been developed by the Michigan Department of Education. At ages three, four, and five your child should be able to accomplish the following:

Walk up stairs, stand momentarily on one foot, ride a tricycle, feed his or her self, open the door, and tell you about toilet needs.

Hop in place; throw a ball over his or her head; catch a bounced ball; copy a circle; point to basic colors; know his or her own sex, age, and last name; begin to play with other children. Four-year-olds should also be able to use sentences with correct grammar such as: "May I go to the store?" or "I want a cookie." Children should be able to wash their hands without assistance.

Walk backward heel to toe, run on tiptoe, and lace their own shoes. Print a few capital letters and recognize his or her own printed name; cut food with a knife; play with others. Five-year-olds should also be able to answer verbally to "Hi" and "How are you?"

If your child is having difficulty in a number of these areas he or she might have special needs. Get in touch with the special education director or the superintendent of your local schools. Your school may have programs available for preschool children with special needs. If not, the school can help you to find agencies in your community that offer the necessary services.

The earlier you recognize your child's special needs and seek help, the more help you can give your child to develop normally. For more information on **Project Find** see *Information Station.*

Another Look:

Am I pushing my child too hard?

Am I doing enough?

Experts have found that you don't need to push your child to learn academic skills at an early age: efforts to do so simply do not work. Children forget most of what is learned if the material is not appropriate to their age and abilities. The best thing parents can do for their preschoolers is to allow their children to play freely.

Young children learn through play and interacting with family members. Allow kids to enjoy this time: **don't push.**

Information Station:

Some books that you might find helpful are:

Caring for Your Baby and Young Child: Birth to Age 5 (American Academy of Pediatrics, 141 Northwest Point Blvd., P.O. Box 927, Elk Grove Village, IL 60009-0927, 1993, $16.45, bulk orders at reduced prices). This valuable reference contains 676 pages with more than 350 illustrations. The first section is a comprehensive parenting manual covering topics from preparing for childbirth and choosing a pediatrician to bonding and basic child care. The second half of the book is an encyclopedic guide to recognizing and dealing with health problems, ranging from common infectious diseases to developmental disabilities and chronic conditions.

How to Talk So Kids Will Listen & Listen So Kids Will Talk, Adele Faber and Elaine Mazlish (Avon Books a division of The Hearst Corporation, 1350 Avenue of the Americas, New York, NY 10019, 1982, $9.00). Parenting book based on the principles of psychologist Hiam Ginott.

The Magic Years: Understanding and Handling the Problems of Early Childhood, Selma Fraiberg (Macmillan, 1966, $11.00). Describes typical problems experienced at each stage of a young child's development. Practical suggestions for how to handle problems.

Parenting Your Toddler: The Experts Guide to the Tough and Tender Years, Patricia H. Shimm and K. Ballen (Addison-Wesley, 1995, $10.00). A guide for 18 months to 3 years from Barnard College Center for Toddler Development. Twenty years of collective wisdom!

The Portable Pediatrician for Parents: A Month-by-Month Guide to Your Child's Physical and Behavioral Development from Birth to Age Five, Laura Walter Nathanson, M.D., FAAP (Harper Perennial, 1994; $20.00). This is a wonderful book. Well worth its price. Combines information about both medical and behavior issues, with lots of reassurance and humor. Dr. Nathanson has been in practice for 20 years.

Touchpoints, T. Berry Brazelton, M.D. (A Merloyd Lawrence Book, Addison Wesley Publishing Company, 170 Fifth Avenue, New York, NY 10010, 1992, $22.95). A comprehensive book on the emotional and behavioral development of young children.

Your Child's Self Esteem, Dorothy Corkille Briggs (Dolphin Books Edition, Doubleday & Co., 1975, $10.95). Step-by-step guidelines for raising responsible, productive, and happy children.

Questions about how your child is developing?

Call your local school principal, county, district or regional school unit or state department of education.
In Michigan contact:
    Project Find
    Michigan Department of Education
    Special Education Services
    P.O. Box 30008
    Lansing, MI 48909
    1-800-252-0052.

Reading, Reading, Reading

At School:

Many parents think that children learn to read in elementary school. In fact, many children know a lot about reading before they even enter kindergarten.

In preschool children learn the sounds of letters and some words. Children also learn about stories, and the basics of what makes up a story, the characters and plot sequence. In both small and larger group settings children are read to by the teacher and discuss the stories.

There are other approaches used as well. In some preschools children invent their own stories and put them on tape. Some teachers read a portion of a story to children and then let the kids decide how the story will end. In other cases, students use puppets to act out stories. All of these approaches help give a child the reasoning and language skills necessary to become a strong reader.

Don't be surprised if your preschooler asks you about specific words and letters or wants you to spell certain words. Of course, don't be surprised if your child wants you to read to him or her!

At Home:

The most important way you can help your preschooler become a strong reader is to read aloud to the child. The influential 1984 report of the Commission on Reading, *Becoming a Nation of Readers: What Parents Can Do,* bluntly states:

> The single most important activity for building the knowledge required for eventual success in reading is reading aloud to children.

Reading to your preschooler doesn't have to mean the traditional bedtime story. Tips for reading aloud to your child will follow in this material, but first think of all the daily opportunities to read to your child. Writing out and then reading a shopping list is great way to introduce your child to the written word. You might even have your child help select items from the list when you shop, or help your child identify the items that go with shopping coupons. Reading and following recipes is another fun way to link words on the page to actual foods. Writing greeting cards is yet another way to get your preschooler involved with reading.

When you do sit down to read a book with your child, start with something simple and fun. Even the most simple books can teach children lessons that will help them learn to read on their own. For example, children learn about the structure of our language, that there are spaces between words, and that the print always goes from left to right.

As you read, point out pictures in the book. Most important, talk with your child about the story. Ask questions about what's going on in the book or ask your child to predict what is going to happen next. You should also relate the book to the child's life as much as possible. If you see a picture of a certain animal, remind your child that he or she may have seen the same animal somewhere else, in the neighborhood, in a book or magazine, or at the zoo.

Getting It Straight:

Reading aloud with your child can be a magical experience. Don't be surprised if your child selects favorite books that he or she wants read over and over. Try leaving out a few words from a page and you'll likely be corrected! Not only is your child learning, he or she is spending intimate time with you that is invaluable for developing self esteem.

Of course, the example you set has a great deal to do with how excited your child becomes about reading. If possible, you should buy a children's dictionary to get your child in the habit of looking words up. Make regular trips to the library. Be sure that your child sees you reading, even if it's just the evening paper or a magazine. You have a powerful influence on your children. If they see you reading for pleasure and for a purpose, they will imitate you. As one three-year-old said, "I'm reading, I just can't say the words!" He was, of course, pretending to read because this was his mother's favorite pastime.

Another Look:

Have you been reading aloud to your child, either stories or in more casual settings? Do you talk about words and stories with your child? Most important, is your child showing interest in reading and words? If you feel there is a problem, contact your child's teacher.

Information Station:

You'll find more information about reading and reading aloud to your child in the following:

Children's Books: Awards and Prizes. (The Children's Book Council.) A compilation of children's books honored throughout the world. A non-evaluative listing, revised every two years. Look for it in the reference section of your library.

Get Ready to Read, Toni S. Gould (Walker and Co., 1991, $12.95). Gould has been a reading consultant for 35 years. Her book is a systematic guide to how to teach reading and when. The activities are fun and suitable for helping your child get ready to read and begin to read. For preschool, kindergarten and first grade teachers and parents.

Growing Up Reading: Learning to Read Through Creative Play, Jill Frankel Hauser (Williamson Publishing, 1993, $12.95). Early months to seven years. The layout, drawings, and photos make this book a pure delight. It's packed with materials and ideas to help adults and kids have fun reading and being together! Guide to books, too. Highly recommended.

Helping Your Child Learn to Read, B. Cullinan & B. Bagert (Consumer Information Center, Pueblo, CO 81009, 1993. Send for free catalog.) One of the wonderful booklets developed by the U.S. Department of Education. Ties in national education goals "by the year 2000 every child will start school ready to learn."

Keys to Your Child's Intellect, Terrel H. Bell (Terrel Bell and Associates, 1814 Woodhaven Circle, Sarasota, FL 34232, 1992, $22.95). This handbook describes techniques and activities on how to expose a child, from infant to age five, to a stimulating, mind-nurturing environment.

The New Read-Aloud Handbook, Jim Trelease (Penguin Books, 1989, $9.95). A million-copy bestseller that shows how every child can become a book lover. Highly recommended.

Reading for the Love of It, Michele Landsburg (Prentice Hall Press, 1989, $10.95). A guide to more than 400 great children's books for children from four to thirteen.

Ready for School? What Every Preschooler Should Know, Marge Eberts and Peggy Gisler (Meadowbrook Press, 1991, $5.95). This well-organized book tells you how to raise children who are curious, communicative, confident and ready to learn when they get to school. It includes a wide range of learning activities geared to the child's age—from birth to five.

RX for Reading, Barbara J. Fox, Ph.D., (Penguin Books, 1989, $7.95). This concise, comprehensive guide shows how you can help add to the reading skills your child is learning in school.

Parent's Choice Foundation, Box 185, Newton, MA 02168; (617) 965-5913, FAX (617) 965-4516. Sponsors of a variety of projects related to the evaluation of children's media. They publish *Parents' Choice*, $18.00 quarterly, "the only nonprofit consumer guide to children's books, toys, video, audio, computer programs, television, magazines and rock 'n' roll."

As a mother who bought *Horn Book* (written for childrens' librarians) the next best resource I've found is the *Chinaberry Catalog* (Chinaberry Book Service, 2780 Via Orange Way, Suite B., Spring Valley, CA 91978, quarterly, free). Over 100 pages with delightful reviews. The reviewers report, "It's no exaggeration to say that for every one book you find in this catalog, we've considered a hundred others." Wonderful. Your author.

Good for You!

The Hows and Whys of Discipline

At School:

Children in preschool learn problem solving skills in health classes. Children learn to talk about their feelings instead of hitting, poking, or pinching. They learn about sharing and cooperating with others. Sharing, listening, and respecting the needs of others are stressed as important aspects of growing up healthy.

Teaching self-discipline is not easy. The most successful preschool programs tend to use methods that:

✔ Focus on cooperation.

✔ Teach problem solving and decision making skills.

✔ Listen to the concerns of the children.

✔ Offer individual support to children when needed.

✔ Accept all feelings. Teach appropriate ways of acting on the feelings expressed.

At Home:

It is important that the adults in a child's life understand the difference between discipline and punishment. Understanding the difference will help you teach your child self-discipline.

> Discipline is setting limits, acting firmly but kindly. Most of all, discipline teaches that actions have consequences.
>
> Punishment is often confused with discipline, but there are real differences between the two. Punishment is hitting, nagging, threatening, lecturing, and name calling. Punishment means control by another person and often hurts, either physically or emotionally.

The job of the family is to help children grow up and be in control of themselves. Punishment doesn't help. In fact, the negative effects of punishment are real and severe. Children will lie or rebel in order to avoid punishment. Studies have shown that the use of physical force results in greater violence in the child. One recent study has even linked harsh authoritarian discipline to a greater risk of substance abuse in later years.

Here are some tips to make discipline easier around your home:

✓ **Set rules in advance.** Try using clear, positive statements. Set a few, important rules that children can remember. Tell children what *to do*, instead of just what *not to do*.

✓ **Allow kids to help create some rules.** "How do you think we can make our mornings go more smoothly?"

✓ **Catch kids being good and praise them.** Your kids will repeat good behavior if they get attention for being good.

✓ **Decide together on what will happen when rules are broken.** Children and adolescents should clearly understand the consequences of breaking the rules.

✓ **Decide together what behaviors will earn special privileges.** Children need to understand the relationship between behaviors and receiving rewards. Remember that the best rewards are attention and praise. These help the child become a person who feels proud. Concrete rewards, like stickers, money, and cookies can be perceived as bribes. These children behave well because they believe there is something in it for them. The bribes may fail to help the children behave well because such behavior is right.

✓ **Explain the reasons for rules.** Yes, it takes time, but it works.

The rules that you set should be appropriate to the ages of your children. A preschooler doesn't act the same way as an adult or older child. Young children especially, have a short attention span. They are attracted to almost everything going on around them. They often have difficulty settling in on a single task. If your child can't sit at the dinner table for more than ten minutes or starts to run through the grocery store when you are out shopping, this does not mean that the child is intentionally misbehaving. More than likely, the child may be acting appropriately for his or her age level.

At Home: (continued)

One of the problems parents face when disciplining children is understanding what is normal behavior and what is not. Young children often lack the verbal skills necessary to express their feelings. Young children also lack the skills to wait or delay getting something they want. This is why a preschooler may grab a toy away from another child or have a temper tantrum. Temper tantrums may also occur when a child is frustrated because he or she can't do a certain task. A good way to deal with this kind of behavior is to use time-outs.

What is Time-Out?

Time-out is a disciplinary method that interrupts inappropriate behavior by removing the child from the "scene of action." By removing the misbehaving child, the parent is being firm but kind while setting limits, and is communicating respect for the child.

Time-out is a calming period which helps children stop the misbehavior and prepare themselves to return to the scene and make choices about future behavior. It also gives parents time to collect themselves and decide what they will say or do, next.

How Does Time-Out Differ From Punishment?

Both the use of the word punishment and its meaning—to cause to undergo pain, loss, or suffering for a crime or wrongdoing—infer an attitude of superiority. "I am angry or disappointed, therefore you are being punished." Naturally children need to experience consequences which may be unpleasant for acts of misbehavior. However, these consequences need not cause pain or suffering.

Therefore we need to think of a consequence as a natural result for an act of misbehavior, which conveys an attitude of instruction and respect. "I am angry because . . . The consequence for your behavior/action is . . ."

Time-out provides a kind, but firm consequence for misbehavior.

How Do I Begin Time-Out?

At around 18 months of age, toddlers can be introduced to a modified time-out. For behaviors like hitting and biting, simply remove the child from the scene of action and state your rule: "People are not for biting."

Between the ages of two and one-half, and three and one-half, your child should be able to understand the words: *calm*, *stop*, and *wait*. During this age span your child can be taught the process of time-out. Clearly explain when and how it will be used. Walk your child through the steps.

(continued on page 14)

13

At Home: (continued)

Time-Out—The Process:

1. **Tell your child when time-out will be used.** Some parents use time-outs for hitting, biting, fighting, swearing, and general lack of cooperation when rules have been clearly stated.

2. **Decide where the time-out area will be.** Show your child.

3. **Give your child the choice,** "When you are able to come back and (cooperate, stop hitting, etc.), you may leave the time-out area."

4. **Enforce the time-out.** This may mean walking your child to the time-out area and/or gently holding him from behind.

5. **Praise or encourage your child immediately after the time-out.** "I'm glad you are playing gently with your brother."

Points to Remember:

1. **Use a tone of voice that shows respect for the child.** Firm, but matter-of-fact. "You have chosen by your behavior to take a time-out," or "Time-out for hitting."

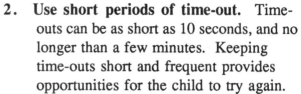

2. **Use short periods of time-out.** Time-outs can be as short as 10 seconds, and no longer than a few minutes. Keeping time-outs short and frequent provides opportunities for the child to try again.

3. **Let your child decide when he is ready to leave time-out and cooperate.** Being able to choose when he is ready to get up and behave appropriately gives your child a deep sense of self-control and independence. He feels your belief and trust that he can learn to control himself.

4. **The time-out area should be far enough away to let the child calm/quiet down, but close enough for him to see what he is missing.** Use an area that works for your child, and one that would not be associated with unpleasant surroundings, such as facing a wall, or sitting in a cold or dark area. Another room works well for some children, for others the separation may be frightening. Simply being asked to time-out in the same room can be very effective for children.

5. **Tell your child that he or she may return to the scene and try again after calming down and finishing any crying, whining, or fussing.**

6. **Redirect the child to an appropriate activity after time-out and comment on appropriate behavior.** "I'm glad you have decided to share your puzzle. I'm pleased to see you smile and play."

RULES

What is Time-Out? modified from the book *I Told You a Million Times ... Building Self-Esteem in Young Children Through Discipline* by Judy Snyder. Copyright © 1989 by Judy Snyder. Reprinted by permission.

Getting It Straight:

Setting rules and limits for your family —and disciplining your child—involves self esteem, both yours and your childs. One easy way to guide yourself through the process is to get in the habit of asking yourself three simple questions about rules for your children.

1) Is this rule to keep my child safe?

2) Is this rule to help my child's self esteem and school performance?

3) Is this rule to keep something from being damaged or destroyed?

The answer should be *yes* to one or more of these questions. Otherwise, the rule is probably not necessary. Remember, the more rules you have, the more time you have to spend enforcing them.

Self-discipline and self esteem go hand in hand. Your preschooler needs a great deal of adult help to avoid the temptation to break rules that seem restrictive or just plain inconvenient. You'll need to be there for your children to remind them of rules and the reasons for rules. However, the benefits to this approach—even if it seems time consuming and tiresome—are enormous for your child's self esteem. If you take the time now, eventually the child will learn self-guidance, saving you time in the long run. Children who have the structure and limits of good discipline at home are more likely to feel good about themselves, succeed in school, and make friends. Most important, these children gradually learn to gain control of their own emotions, feelings, and behavior. This is what is called self-discipline.

Another Look:

What is the difference between discipline and punishment? Discipline teaches, punishment hurts. What are your expectations for your children? What changes would you like in their behavior? Is your child actually misbehaving? Or is the behavior due to the child's age and stage of development?

Information Station:

Check with your local school district to see if parenting classes are offered. One popular program is STEP (Systematic Training for Effective Parenting). This program is based upon the principle of democratic discipline that allows children to participate in developing family rules and practice decision making skills.

There are many books that are available on parenting and discipline. Some books that you might find helpful are:

Fathers and Toddlers by Jean Marzollo (Harper Perennial, 1994, $10.00). Easy, non-threatening, fun guide to children between the ages of 18 months and 3. Positive ideas, wonderful drawings. Educationally sound.

Good Parents for Hard Times, Joanne Barbara Koch and Linda Nancy Freeman, M.D. (Simon and Schuster, Rockefeller Center, 1230 Avenue of the Americans, New York, NY, 1992, $10.00). Helps parents understand and cope with the challenges of childhood. Practical advice on recognizing emotional difficulties and helping children through tough times. Helps a child develop self esteem and good decision making skills.

How to Teach Your Children Discipline, Marilyn E. Gootman (National Committee for Prevention of Child Abuse, P.O. Box 94284, Chicago, IL 60690; 312-663-3520; 35 cents). Alternatives to spanking, tips on problem solving and ways to calm down when feeling out of control.

I Told You a Million Times, Judy Snyder (Family Connection Publications, P.O. Box 406, Cary, IL 60013, 1989, $5.95 + $1.25 postage). This book is excellent. Provides very concrete information in a clear way to help you discipline your young children.

If We'd Wanted Quiet We Would Have Raised Goldfish. Poems selected by Bruce Lansky. (Meadowbrook Press, 1994, $12.00). This is a book of poems that parents can understand and enjoy. Poems from birth to aging: you'll read these over and over *and* give the book to friends.

Love and Learn: Discipline for Young Children by Alice S. Honig (National Association for the Education of Young Children, 1834 Connecticut Ave. N.W., Washington, DC 20009, 1989, 50¢). A gem of a pamphlet. Eleven panels give an excellent bird's-eye-view of how children grow and learn, by a leading educator.

Pick Up Your Socks . . . And Other Skills Growing Children Need, Elizabeth Crary (Parenting Press, 1990, $11.95). Examples and exercises for teaching children responsibility for housework, homework, and personal safety.

To Listen to a Child: Understanding the Normal Problems of Growing Up, T. Berry Brazelton (Addison-Wesley, 1992, $10.95). Describes normal child development and behaviors.

Good for You!

Kids Learn to Recycle

At School:

Your child is learning in health classes that to be healthy means guarding the environment around them. These lessons are called Caring for My Environment. Children learn practical skills which involve recycling, saving, and planting. One of many objects they will learn to recycle are toys. The children and their teacher will set up a Toy Exchange.

17

At Home:

You can participate in the Toy Exchange by providing toys, books, and games (all the pieces, if possible) that your family no longer needs. Don't worry if the toys are not in working order. One of the lessons taught is to try to fix the toys so they can be used again.

Children will need sacks to carry home their traded goods. If you don't have extra toys or books around your child will be included anyway.

Perhaps an adult in your household would like to help with the recycling project. Children love to have adults from their family in the classroom. And, studies show children do better when families come to school and help in the classroom.

Perhaps you visit garage sales to obtain play things and clothes for your children. This is recycling too and children would enjoy hearing about your bargains. Do contact your child's teacher to find out about all the recycling projects going on in class.

Getting It Straight:

Children develop a sense of responsibility when they contribute to keeping our environment clean. They need to learn that the safety of all living things depends on conserving the natural and physical resources of the planet. When children work on projects to care for the earth, including recycling projects, they feel strong, important, and competent. They feel they make a difference.

Another Look:

Have you talked with your child's teacher about the recycling lessons taught at school? Many objects can be recycled and saved. What is your family recycling? Have you taken your child to visit the recycling center in your community?

Information Station:

Visit your local library and ask the children's librarian to help you find books about recycling.

Here Comes the Recycling Truck!, Meyer Seltzer (Albert Whitman & Company, 1992, $13.95).

Recyclying (A New True Book), Joan Kalbacken and Emilie Lepthien (Childrens Press, Inc., 1991, $4.95).

What Can You Make Of It?, Franz Bradenberg (Greenwillow Books, 1977).

Conflict Resolution: Violence

At School:

The world of your child in a preschool program and the world of TV are very different.

At school, children talk about conflicts occurring over shared space, objects, or ideas. This type of conflict is very familiar to families. Kids fight, bicker, squabble, or tattle. In school, your child is taught that everyone involved usually has an idea on how to solve the conflict. Children learn that it is a good idea for everyone to stop and listen. Kids find out that usually the best solution is one that is ok with everyone. This can take a lot of compromising and changing your mind, especially for four-year-olds! Once the compromise takes place, the teacher helps your child try out solutions and practice ways of keeping life peaceful for everybody. Sounds easy, doesn't it? But every parent knows how much practice this takes.

At Home:

Children begin watching cartoons on TV around the age of two. By the age of six about 90 percent have developed a television habit. Children love cartoons because every action is highlighted with attention-getting features and the sounds draw them back to the action.

The late John Condry, professor of Human Development and Family Studies at Cornell University, said that when young children see violence they may think that "might makes right." He reports that children are unlikely to understand the subtle messages of the cartoon—for example that certain actions are more justified than others. What kids *do* get is the message that if you want something and have a greater power, you get what you want. Condry says that the action/adventure cartoons children watch are stories of power. A recent study, for example, found an average of 25 acts of violence per hour in children's programming.

At Home: (continued)

How do stories of violence and power influence children's behavior? Studies show that children who are heavy viewers of TV are more aggressive than those who are light viewers. Viewing violent TV not only affects children's behavior but their attitudes, beliefs, and values. Condry reports that heavy viewers are not sensitive to violence, they are less moved by it, and less responsive to it. Four hours per day is considered heavy viewing for young children.

Here are some tips to help children develop good television-viewing habits:

1) Keep a record of how many hours of TV your children watch, and what they watch. Generally, it's good to limit viewing to two hours or less per day.

2) Learn about current TV programs and videos and be selective. Select TV programs and videos meaningful to your family. Some TV programs you may wish to consider include *"Mr. Rogers' Neighborhood," "Sesame Street," "Shining Time Station," "Long Ago and Far Away," "Lambchop's Play-Along"* and *"Barney and Friends"*—all from public broadcasting. You may also find quality shows on cable on the Disney or Nickelodeon channels.

3) If you have a VCR, you may wish to seek out videos made by Linda Ellerbee's Lucky Duck Productions. Of course, videos vary in quality, but versions of classic children's books, such as *Babar* or *Snow White* are a good place to start.

4) Plan with your children (starting at age 3) what programs to watch. After selecting programs appropriate for your children, help them decide which ones to watch. Turn the TV on when these shows start, and turn the TV off when the show is over.

5) Watch television with your children so you can talk about the program. Pay special attention to how children respond to the program so that you can later talk about what they saw.

6) Follow up TV viewing with activities or games. You might have your child tell you a new word he or she learned on television that you can look up together in the dictionary. Or you might have him or her make up his or her own story about one of his or her favorite TV characters.

Getting it Straight:

How can young children ever learn how to solve problems and conflicts if television scripts have an average sentence length between four and six words? According to Priscilla Vail, author of *Smart Kids With School Problems,* heavy television viewing can slow down intellectual and language development that is needed for solving problems, developing imagination and creativity. "These short TV messages try to provide instant solutions to complicated problems," says Steven Spector, Ph.D., Beacon Hill Clinic, Birmingham, Michigan.

Another Look:

Have you made a simple chart for the refrigerator that lists the shows your 4-year-old watches and the total hours watched per day? Have you avoided the use of TV for babysitting?

Information Station:

Parents who would like help in finding good TV programs for children can subscribe to *Parents' Choice,* a quarterly review of children's media. Write to Parents' Choice Foundation, Box 185, Newton, MA 02168. A subscription is $18 a year. A sample copy is $2.

Helping Your Child Get Ready for School, Nancy Paulu (U.S. Dept. of Education, Office of Educational Research and Improvement, 1992, $3.25 includes shipping and handling). Order by writing to the Superintendent of Documents, P.O. Box 371954, Pittsburgh, PA 15250-7954. Excellent.

"Developmentally Appropriate Television: Putting Children First," Diane E. Levin and Nancy Carlsson-Page. *Young Children*, July, 1994. (National Association for the Education of Young Children, 1509 16th Street N.W., Washington, DC 20036-1426. For a reprint of the 7 page article send $5.00 to N.A.E.Y.C.) A superb review of the effects of TV on young children, what children are learning while "glued to the screen," and what can be done to counteract the influence of TV. Resources and references. Parents can also read this helpful article at their library.

Feelings and Faces

At School:

Children are learning about feelings in health classes in preschool. Their teacher will talk about how children express pleasant feelings such as happiness or excitement (giving hugs, smiling, laughing). The teacher also tells children that it is important to express unpleasant emotions. Children are urged to tell grownups they trust if they feel unhappy, uncomfortable, scared, or worried. They are told to talk to parents, grandparents, teachers, and other adults they trust.

Children will learn that there are many ways for them to find out how someone else is feeling. They discover that people tell us their feelings by how they hold their bodies, with their faces, and with words. "It is words," the teacher says, "that are usually more clear than other kinds of messages." Children practice using feeling words and learn, for example, how to use words if they are bothered by another child. They learn to say, "Please move over and sit in your own spot," if someone is leaning on them at story time.

These lessons about feelings are important since children understand how to feel more relaxed, calm, or comfortable. Children are taught how to recognize stress. They learn that when they feel stress they should put their energy into riding their bikes, talking to the teacher, or going to the quiet corner in the room. These teachings set a firm base for handling conflict without hitting, fighting, or bickering.

At Home:

Families want children to learn how to control their anger and other emotions both at school and home. Sometimes a problem at school may leave emotions that carry over at home. Likewise, if your family is having a tough time with a problem, you may wish to alert your child's teacher so that he or she can be especially caring and helpful to your child. It isn't always possible to leave problems and the emotions that come from upsetting situations either in the play corner at school or on the kitchen table at home.

A Feelings and Faces Game

You can help your child learn more about feelings with this game.

You will need a stack of newspapers or magazines, scissors, card board, and paste.

You can make paste by mixing one-half cup flour moistened with water until you get a glue-like texture.

Here are four feeling faces:

CALM   HAPPY   SURPRISED   UPSET

Help your child cut out pictures to illustrate these four feelings. Paste the photos on four separate card boards. If you have time, continue to find more photos to show the four emotions.

1) Ask your child to turn over all the photos mounted on the cards.

2) Turn one card face up. Say that you will guess which one of the feelings is in the first photo.

3) Have a discussion about the photo on the first card.

4) Ask your child to guess which photo is being turned up on the second card.

5) Take turns and continue turning up the cards and talking about each one until you have talked about all four emotions.

6) Put the cards away for another time.

You can use this game to talk to your child when he or she is having difficulty telling you about feelings.

Getting It Straight:

Children who have learned to handle stress may be less likely to turn to unhealthy substances later. They may avoid cigarettes, drugs, and alcohol as ways to relieve stress.

Another Look:

Do you believe your child understands that it is acceptable to express emotions even if they are unpleasant ones such as jealousy, envy, or anger?

Information Station:

My Book About Alcohol and *My Book About Drugs*, both coloring books are produced by the Michigan Substance Abuse and Traffic Safety Information Center (2409 East Michigan, Lansing, MI 48912-4019, 517-482-9902 or 1-800-626-INFO; free).

Ready for School: What Every Preschooler Should Know, Marge Eberts and Peggy Gisler (Meadowbrook Press, 1991, $5.95) Helpful suggestions from former teachers about children from birth to five.

The *Feelings* series developed in England consists of six excellent books about feelings. Try reading one of these books to your preschooler. *Feelings:* [1] *Afraid* - [2] *Angry* - [3] *Hurt* - [4] *Jealous* - [5] *Lonely* - [6] *Sad*, Janine Amos (Raintree Press, 1991, $3.95 each). A beautiful series to read to your preschooler.

Good for You!

Healthy Futures

At School and At Home:

It is essential that families and schools work together to provide a healthy future for all children. All families want their children to be free of disease. Follow the Immunization Schedule included on page 30. Your children must meet Michigan's immunization requirements to enroll in any nursery, day care, preschool, or Head Start program, and public or non-public schools.

If you have more than one child under four please ask us for copies of this material for each child.

Getting it Straight:

Provisions of the Vaccines for Children Program:

✓ The new law provides that all uninsured, Medicaid-eligible, and Native-American children age 18 and under, will be eligible for free vaccines through any participating provider.

✓ Children may receive their vaccinations from their pediatrician, community health clinic, or other provider of health care. It will not be necessary to go to public clinics in order to receive free vaccines.

✓ In addition, children without insurance coverage for vaccines—even if they have some health insurance—who seek services at community and migrant health centers and homeless health care clinics can receive free vaccines.

✓ The program presently includes all immunizations that are recommended by the United States Centers for Disease Control.

For more information on the Vaccines for Children Program, contact Michigan Department of Public Health at (517) 335-8159.

Call National Vaccines for Children Program, 1-800-232-7468 for information about services in states other than Michigan.

Immunization is More Than a One Shot Deal . . . (Michigan Department of Public Health, 3423 N. Logan St., P.O. Box 30195, Lansing, MI 48909 or call 517-335-8159; 1994; free.)

Good for You!

Schedule For
Early Vaccinations

Call your doctor, a clinic in your neighborhood, or your local Health Department for times and places to get your child immunized.

My child's name: _____

My child will be:

2 months old in the month of: _____

4 months old in the month of: _____

6 months old in the month of: _____

15 months old in the month of: _____

4 years old in the month of: _____

This is your personal schedule for the important, early vaccinations your child will need to have before the age of four.

HANG THIS SCHEDULE ON YOUR REFRIGERATOR AS AN EARLY REMINDER

Immunization for All

Beginning in October 1994, all children in this country will be able to receive free immunization against infectious diseases.

Legislation enacted in 1993 created the Vaccines for Children Program that will provide free vaccines to more than 10.6 million preschool children.

Your Child's Immunization Schedule

Is your child getting his or her vaccines on time? Follow this immunization schedule recommended by the Michigan Department of Public Health.

	DTP (Diphtheria Tetanus & Pertussis Vaccine)	OPV (Live Oral Polio Vaccine and Drops)	MMR (Measles Mumps, & Rubella Vaccine)	Hib (Haemo-philus b Conjugate Vaccine)	Hep B Hepatitis B	Td Tetanus Diphtheria
Birth					✓	
1 month					✓	
2 months	✓	✓		✓		
4 months	✓	✓		✓		
6 months	✓	✓		✓	✓	
12-15 months	✓		✓	✓		
4-6 years (before school entry)	✓	✓	✓			
14-16 years (every 10 years)						✓

Other schedules are possible.
Consult your local health department or family doctor.

For more information on the location of the Public Health clinic nearest you, call: 1-961-BABY (961-2229) or
1-800-26BIRTH (262-4784)

Good for You!

Taking Care of Your Child's Teeth

At School:

In preschool health classes children are learning about good grooming and about keeping their bodies clean. Children are learning about the importance of their teeth and how to take care of their teeth by brushing properly, flossing, eating healthy foods, and making regular visits to the dentist.

Children learn that healthy teeth serve several purposes besides making a beautiful smile. Teeth are used to:

✓ Chew and digest food.
✓ Talk and form words.
✓ Hold spaces for permanent teeth. If baby teeth are lost too early, permanent teeth may come in crooked.

Some activities your child may be doing in school to learn about their teeth include: songs about brushing, drawing or painting a mouth, and play-acting a visit to a dentist's office. Some teachers may invite a dentist or dental hygienist to visit the class or schedule a field trip to a dentist's office.

At Home:

Brush,Brush, Brush; Floss,Floss, Floss!

The best way to teach your child good dental health habits is to set a good example. Your child can grow up free of cavities, but he or she will need your help. You can begin to teach your child good dental habits by letting him or her watch you brush and floss.

At Home: (continued)

Children are capable of brushing their own teeth by age two or three. Flossing should begin at this time, too. You should always re-brush and re-floss your preschool child's teeth to ensure a thorough cleaning.

Disclosing tablets are a fun way to check for spots that might have been missed during brushing. These tablets contain a harmless color that sticks to plaque on the teeth (plaque is a soft, sticky film containing bacteria). Your child can then see the color and brush away the plaque. Dentists and pharmacists can provide these tablets.

Although your child's baby teeth will be replaced by permanent teeth, they are still very important to a healthy mouth. If baby teeth decay, an infection may result that can damage the permanent teeth that are still in the gums.

FOOD GUIDE PYRAMID
•A GUIDE TO DAILY FOOD CHOICES FOR PRESCHOOLERS•

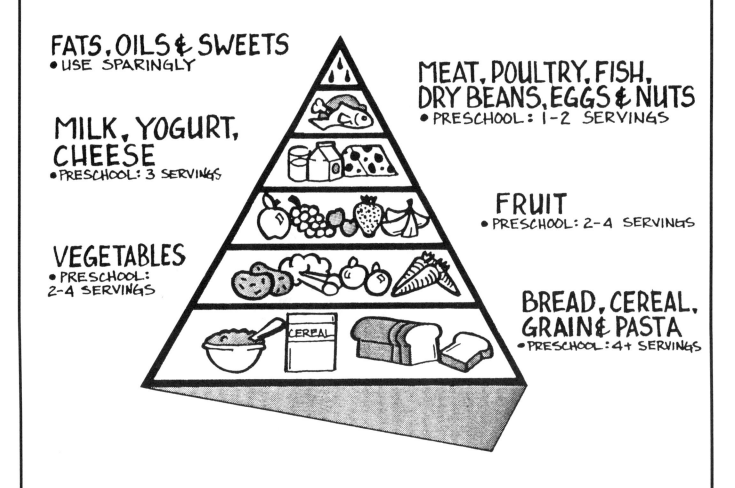

FATS, OILS & SWEETS
•USE SPARINGLY

MEAT, POULTRY, FISH, DRY BEANS, EGGS & NUTS
•PRESCHOOL: 1-2 SERVINGS

MILK, YOGURT, CHEESE
•PRESCHOOL: 3 SERVINGS

FRUIT
•PRESCHOOL: 2-4 SERVINGS

VEGETABLES
•PRESCHOOL: 2-4 SERVINGS

BREAD, CEREAL, GRAIN & PASTA
•PRESCHOOL: 4+ SERVINGS

Eating Right

What kids eat is important to keeping their teeth healthy. Foods loaded with sugar, such as sugar-coated cereals, candy, cookies, ice cream, and cake, increase the possibility of your child getting cavities.

The chart on page 32 will help you understand the types of food and the number of servings per day that your child needs to be healthy. Remember that preschoolers eat servings one-half the size of adult servings. Healthy snacks count as servings, too.

Let's Keep Teeth Strong!

The time of day that food is eaten.

Foods that are eaten just before bedtime can stay on the teeth throughout the night. Therefore, it is not a good idea to give your child milk and cookies just before bedtime. Try giving children cheese or popcorn or unsweetened fruit drinks instead.

The length of time that food is in the mouth.

Foods that your kids suck on, such as hard candy, stay in the mouth for a long time. This causes acids to attack the teeth for longer periods of time. Sugary drinks that are sipped over a long period of time have the same effect. Have your child brush as soon as possible after eating these foods.

Tips for Making Your Child's Visit to the Dentist Easier:

Be Positive!

If you are afraid of the dentist—don't pass that fear to your child. Don't tell your child "this isn't going to hurt." Statements like that only make your child suspect that something painful is going to happen. Tell your child that the dentist is a friendly doctor who will help him or her stay healthy.

Read Your Child A Book

You can help prepare your child for their first visit to the dentist by reading a book about going to the dentist. You and your child will enjoy this time together and at the same time you are preparing your youngster for what to expect at the dentist's office. See *Information Station* for some suggestions.

Visit The Dentist's Office Before Your Child's Appointment

Take your child along when you or another family member visits the dentist. This gives your child a good opportunity to see the office and meet the dentist and dental hygienist.

Scheduling Your Child's Appointment

Make the appointment for the time of day that your child is the most rested. Many children feel the most rested in the morning. If your child is more alert in the afternoon, schedule an afternoon appointment. Be sure to allow plenty of time to get ready. You don't want your child to feel rushed. Feeling rushed may make your child feel upset while at the dentist's office.

Don't Expect Perfect Behavior

Even though you have done your best to prepare your child for their visit to the dentist, your child may still be afraid and misbehave. Sometimes the parent or dentist can talk to the child and calm his or her fears. If this does not work, it may be best to reschedule the visit for another time.

What to do if your child breaks or knocks out a tooth

Your child may knock out a tooth while playing, break a tooth while chewing on a pencil, or while biting on hard food. Here is what to do:

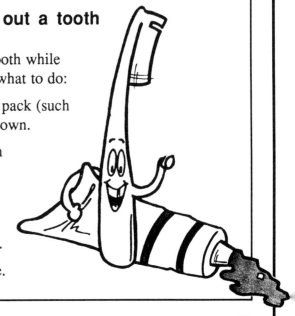

✓ Clean the injured area with warm water and use a cold pack (such as ice cubes wrapped in a cloth) to keep the swelling down.

✓ Save any pieces of the broken tooth. Broken pieces can sometimes be bonded back on to the broken tooth.

✓ Handle the tooth by the top, not by the roots.

✓ Gently rinse the tooth—do not scrub. Place the tooth in a glass of water or milk, or wrap it in a damp towel.

✓ Get to a dentist within thirty minutes, if at all possible.

Getting It Straight:

Tooth decay is the major cause of tooth loss in children. Many dental problems that occur later in life can be prevented by teaching good dental health habits to your children. Follow these steps recommended by the American Dental Association for a lifetime of healthy teeth:

Brush and Floss Regularly

Children should brush their teeth at least twice a day—once in the morning and once at bedtime. Brush after lunch and snacks whenever possible.

Use A Proper Toothbrush

Use a soft-bristled, nylon toothbrush. Be sure that the toothbrush is child-sized. Replace the toothbrush every few months or whenever the bristles begin to fray.

Use Fluoride Toothpaste

Fluoride is a nutrient that helps to strengthen teeth and fight cavities. Most drinking water contains fluoride. However, if the water in your area does not have fluoride, ask your dentist about fluoride supplements. Use fluoride toothpaste when you brush.

Foods to Avoid

Avoid foods that are sticky or chewy, high in sugars and starches, or that stay in your child's mouth a long time. Other foods to avoid include hard candy, dried fruits, and caramels.

Regular Checkups With Your Dentist

Many dentists recommend that your child should be seen for his or her first visit by age two. Continue checkups every six months.

Sealants

A sealant is a thin, plastic coating that is painted on the chewing surfaces of the back teeth, or molars. Although your child's molars will not come in until age 6 or 7, you might want to discuss the benefits of sealants with your dentist.

Getting It Straight:

(continued)

Eat Healthy Foods

Below is a list of nutritious snacks that are good for your child:

- Fruit juices, unsweetened drinks

- Skim or 1% milk

- Frozen desserts such as sherbet, sorbet, fruit ice, popsicles, ice milk, frozen yogurt

- Gingersnaps

- Homemade cookies made with reduced fat and sugar

- Fresh fruit, canned fruit with natural juices

- Vegetable sticks

- Air-popped popcorn

- Pretzels

- Peanut butter in celery sticks

- Low fat cheese (Kids love cheese—and it's good for their teeth, too!)

Another Look:

Have you scheduled a visit to the dentist for your child? What are some healthy snacks that you can give your children? Are you giving your child fruit or carrot sticks instead of cookies or candy? Have you thought of plain popcorn as a great healthy, crunchy snack? Have you posted a chart in a handy place to keep track of your child's brushing? Your child will enjoy coloring in a square each time he or she brushes.

Information Station:

Check with your dentist or local health department for free pamphlets on dental health.

There are many books available on dental health for children. Visit your local library with your child to select some books about visiting the dentist or brushing teeth. Some books that you might find helpful are:

A Trip to the Dentist, Margot Linn and Catherine Siracusa (Harper and Rowe, 10 East 53rd St., New York, NY 10022, 1988, $9.95). For children ages two to five. Explains who will examine Annie's teeth, what the dentist's chair is like and helps answer a young child's questions about what happens in a dentist's office.

Healthy Snacks, Susan Hodges (Warren Publishing House, Inc., P.O. Box 2250, Everett, WA 98203, 1994; $6.95). More than 90 recipes that provide parents, teachers, and day care providers with healthy alternatives to junk-food snacks. Each recipe is low in fat, sugar, and sodium. Complete nutritional information is given for each recipe.

Protecting Our Children's Teeth, Malcom Foster, D.D.S. (Insight Books, a division of Plenum Publishing Corporation, 233 Spring Street, New York, NY 10013, 1992; $23.95). A guide to dental care from infancy through age 12.

The Portable Pediatrician for Parents, Laura Walther Nathanson, M.D., FAAP (HarperCollins Publishers, 1994; $20.00). This book was written by a pediatrician who has been in practice for 20 years and provides a month-by-month guide to your child's physical *and* behavioral development from birth to age five. There are 16 entries about teeth from age infant to five. Outstanding source.

> Request information on children's dental health by sending a self-addressed stamped envelope to:
>
> The American Dental Association
> 211 East Chicago Avenue
> Chicago, Illinois 60611

Peanut Butter and Jelly Days: Feeding My Friends

At School:

In health classes at school, preschool children are playing games and completing projects that are a great deal of fun because they include eating! Children talk about choosing healthy foods and may even prepare healthy snacks for their classmates.

Children will build the new food triangle like the one shown on page 41. Your child will be introduced to the idea of eating different quantities of food. The widest base in the triangle contains breads, cereals, grains and pastas. Children learn that they should eat most of their food from this food group. They also learn that next on the triangle are fruits and vegetables and that they should eat plenty of these foods, too.

Children are taught that a variety of foods are important to their health. The number of servings of each kind of food to eat each day is also talked about. Children even learn the word *nutrient* and find out that sweets and fats have few, if any nutrients.

At Home:

For good health, everyone in the family should eat foods from each group on the triangle each day .

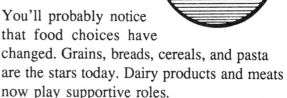

You'll probably notice that food choices have changed. Grains, breads, cereals, and pasta are the stars today. Dairy products and meats now play supportive roles.

The change in recommended foods is because Americans eat too much meat and too many dairy products. Fat has been named as the biggest health risk in our diet.

For years doctors have known that eating too many meals of fatty meat, whole-fat dairy products, rich desserts, and fried foods can cause heart disease and strokes. Scientists are now linking many cancers to a high-fat diet. In addition, fats and sweets are high in calories, but low in nutrients.

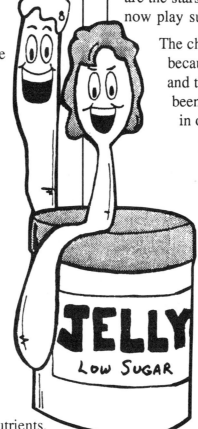

JELLY
LOW SUGAR

At Home: (continued)

In general, families should try to eat less fat, more fruits and vegetables, and more high-fiber foods. Fiber is found in fruits, vegetables, whole-grain cereals and breads, bran, peas, and beans.

Here is a game to help your child understand that many different foods make up a healthy diet.

After your next trip to the grocery store, when you are putting away the groceries, spend an extra five minutes sorting the products you purchased according to the groups on the food triangle we have provided.

Fats, Oils, Sweets
Meat, Poultry, Fish, Dry Beans, Nuts
Milk, Yogurt, Cheese
Fruit
Vegetables
Bread, Cereal, Grain, Pasta

Use the food triangle provided and have your child put a check in the space for each vegetable or fruit you have purchased. Do this for each food you have brought home.

Have your child color the food triangle and post it on your refrigerator for a reference.

Getting it Straight:

Remember that servings for preschoolers are half the size of adult food servings. Therefore, a serving of bread would be one-half slice; of fruit or vegetables, one-quarter cup; and of milk, one-half cup. A preschooler only needs two to four ounces of meat each day. One-to-two servings of poultry, fish, beans, eggs, or nuts can be substituted for meat. Beans have no fat and can be eaten in greater quantities than meat.

Children need to eat five to seven times a day because their stomachs are small and cannot hold much food.

Another Look:

Has your family talked about eating less fats and sweets? Are you providing your family with low fat snacks like fruit, animal crackers, vanilla wafers, popsicles made from fruit juice, graham crackers, gingersnaps, or non-fat yogurt?

38

Information Station:

For Adults:

Basic Nutrition Facts: A Nutrition Reference, Judith V. Anderson and Marian R. Van-Nierop, editors (Attn: Della Jones, Michigan Department of Public Health, Division of Research and Development, 3423 N. Logan St., P.O. Box 30195, Lansing, MI 48909; one copy free to Michigan residents).

Food for Healthy Little Hearts and Recipes for Low-fat Low Cholesterol Meals (American Heart Association of Michigan, 16310 W. 12 Mile Rd., P.O. Box 160, Lathrup Village, MI 48076, 313-557-9500 or 1-800-632-7587; free).

How to Get Your Kids to Eat . . . But Not Too Much, Ellyn Satter (Bull Publishing, 1987, $14.95). How to avoid fights about food, handle children who won't eat, over eat, or won't try new foods.

How Should I Feed My Child: From pregnancy to preschool, S. K. Nissenberg, M. L. Bogle, E. P. Langholz and A. C. Wright (Chronimed Publishing, 1993, $12.95). Registered dietitians, all mothers, have translated scientific facts into a common sense approach to feeding young children. 50 recipes. Outstanding help.

For Children:

Kevin and the School Nurse, Martina Davison; developed by the American Medical Association (AMA) (Random House, 1992, $2.25). Don't be put off by the title; this wonderful, inexpensive book tells the story of a boy who felt weak after not eating properly all day—and what the school nurse and family did. Full color, charming illustrations. Also: *Rita Goes to the Hospital; Robby Visits the Doctor; Maggie and the Emergency Room* all developed by AMA. Useful, culturally sensitive, and fun for kids.

Cholesterol in Children: Healthy Eating is a Family Affair (National Cholesterol Education Program NHLBI Information Center, P.O. Box 30150, Bethesda, Maryland 20824-0105; free). This 51 page book is part of an excellent series. For children ages 2-7 and their family. Booklets are also available for children ages 7-10, 11-14, and 15-18.

Extra Cheese, Please, Cris Peterson, photographed by Alvis Upitis (Boyds Mills Press, $13.95). This story of mozzarella's journey from cow to pizza is as fresh and delicious a slice of information as you'll find for your child. One reason this book works so well is that Peterson lives on a 40-holstein dairy farm in the middle of Wisconsin dairy country.

FOOD GUIDE PYRAMID

•A GUIDE TO DAILY FOOD CHOICES FOR PRESCHOOLERS•

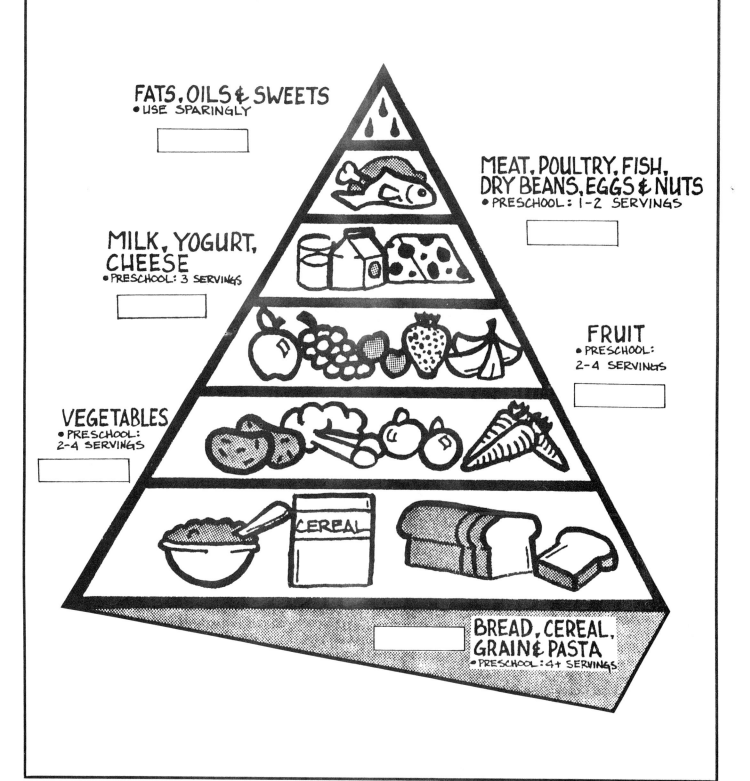

FATS, OILS & SWEETS
•USE SPARINGLY

MEAT, POULTRY, FISH, DRY BEANS, EGGS & NUTS
•PRESCHOOL: 1-2 SERVINGS

MILK, YOGURT, CHEESE
•PRESCHOOL: 3 SERVINGS

FRUIT
•PRESCHOOL: 2-4 SERVINGS

VEGETABLES
•PRESCHOOL: 2-4 SERVINGS

BREAD, CEREAL, GRAIN & PASTA
•PRESCHOOL: 4+ SERVINGS

Good for You!

Smoke Free Me

At School:

Your child is learning in health classes in preschool to take care of their lungs by keeping harmful things out of the lungs. The health lessons include a discussion about smoking cigarettes and how smoking may seem like fun but is a dangerous habit to start.

Your youngster may bring home a poster that carries the message NO SMOKING. The teacher may also distribute these posters to the library or civic center in your community.

Children are beginning to understand the concept of secondhand smoke, the smoke which comes from someone else smoking or just tobacco burning. Children are told that other peoples' smoke is harmful and can get into their bodies. Children learn to move away from smokers, or to politely ask smokers to put out their cigarettes.

At Home:

Secondhand smoke, the smoke given off from burning tobacco or exhaled from the lungs of smokers, has been classified by the U.S. Environmental Protection Agency (EPA) as a known cause of lung cancer. Exposure to secondhand smoke, known as passive smoking, also aggravates asthma. Even among children without asthma, a team of researchers found that acute respiratory illnesses happen twice as often to young children whose parents smoke around them as compared to those with non-smoking parents.

Secondhand smoke has an especially bad effect on infants and toddlers whose parents smoke. A number of studies show that in their first two years of life, babies of parents who smoke at home have a much higher rate of lung diseases such as bronchitis and pneumonia than babies with non-smoking parents.

Ideas to Help Lower the Risk of Passive Smoking

For Nonsmokers:

• Don't allow others to smoke in your home. Let family, friends, co-workers, and others know that smoking is not allowed inside your home.

• Find out about the smoking policies of day-care providers, preschools, and other caregivers. Consider how these policies affect your child's health.

• Ask to sit as far from smokers as possible in restaurants.

• Know the smoking laws in your community. Don't be hesitant to see that these laws are enforced.

• Suggest no-smoking resolutions at organization meetings.

For Smokers:

• Don't smoke around children.

• Increase ventilation by opening windows and using exhaust fans.

• Smoke outside.

Getting it Straight:

About 175,000 children in Michigan have asthma, according to the American Lung Association. One of the most common triggers of asthma is secondhand smoke.

Three hundred ninety thousand (390,000) Americans die each year from the effects of cigarette smoking.

Smoking is responsible for 16% (1 in 6) of all deaths in the United States each year.

According to the Environmental Protection Agency and Centers for Disease Control and Prevention, secondhand smoke causes 3,000 deaths each year from lung cancer, 150,000 to 300,000 cases of bronchitis and pneumonia in youngsters and asthma attacks in more than twice that number.
The New York Times, 3/26/94

Contact your local American Lung Association for help to stop smoking.

Another Look:

Even if you don't quit smoking (or if you don't smoke), have you talked with your child about how easy it is to start and how hard it is to quit smoking? The nicotine in tobacco is very addictive.

Information Station:

Facts About Secondhand Smoke; Facts About Cigarette Smoking; Facts About Nicotine Addiction and Cigarettes. All free from the American Lung Association of Michigan, 403 Seymour Ave., Lansing, MI 48933-1179, or call 1-800-678-5864 or 517-484-4541, 9-5 weekdays.

Growing Up Drug Free: A Parent's Guide to Prevention. To order this guide free of charge, call the Department of Education at 1-800-624-0100 or write to: Growing Up Drug Free, Pueblo, CO 81009.

HIV/AIDS

At School:

In preschool health classes children begin to learn how to take care of their bodies. Children learn that germs are something they can't see but can make them sick. Colds, diarrhea, and strep throat are frequently caused by germs. Children learn that good health habits, such as frequent hand washing, can prevent germs from spreading and from making them sick.

Children also learn that bodily waste and bodily fluids, such as saliva and mucus, also contain germs. Children are taught to wash their hands after they have had contact with germs before eating, touching other people, or playing with toys. For example, your child will learn the importance of washing his or her hands after going to the bathroom, blowing his or her nose, or playing with pets.

PLEASE WASH HANDS BEFORE EATING.

SOAP

At School: (continued)

Another important lesson children learn is what should and should not go into their bodies. Food, water, and medicines given by a doctor, parent, or other health professional are taught to be the only substances that should go into a child's body.

These lessons will help prepare your child to learn about Human Immunodeficiency Virus (HIV) and Acquired Immunodeficiency Syndrome (AIDS) and other communicable diseases when he or she enters elementary school.

What Kids Need to Know About AIDS

Public Act 139 requires AIDS education in every Michigan school, *kindergarten through twelfth grade.* The following is a summary of topics that may be taught at each grade level:

Grades K-6

K   How health workers are trying to prevent the spread of HIV/AIDS.

1   How HIV/AIDS are not spread and how to act toward people with HIV/AIDS.

3   How HIV/AIDS is contracted in comparison with other communicable diseases.

4-6   How HIV affects the immune system; how HIV is and is not transmitted.

Grades 7-12

7-8   How to prevent HIV and Sexually Transmitted Diseases (STDs) by avoiding high risk behaviors such as unprotected sex and intravenous drug use.

9-10   How AIDS is similar to and different from other communicable diseases; levels of infection. HIV disease is both an infectious disease as well as a chronic disease. HIV disease moves on a continuum from *not* having symptoms to *having* symptoms, to death. Death comes usually in 10-12 years depending on the decrease of the function of the immune system, over time.

11-12   How to identify and reduce high risk situations; AIDS testing; facts, myths, and unknowns about AIDS; the ethical, political, and economic issues surrounding AIDS.

The law allows local school boards to decide how HIV/AIDS prevention will be taught in their district. Check with your local school board for more information regarding the policy in your district.

At Home:

Keep the lines of communication open!

Many parents feel uncomfortable talking to their kids about HIV/AIDS. Don't worry if you don't have all of the answers. How you respond to your child's question is just as important as what you say. Keep the lines of communication open! Encourage your child to come to you with their questions on any topic. This can form the foundation for a trusting relationship in later years.

Keep it simple!

Your preschooler does not need or want a detailed, scientific explanation about HIV/AIDS. Keep your answers simple. If you do not know the answer to a question, don't panic. Admit that you don't know the answer and tell your child that you will find the answer as soon as you can.

Experts from the Parent HIV/AIDS Project at Cornell University give the following advice on answering your child's questions about AIDS:

● Understand the meaning behind your child's questions about AIDS. The main concern of young children is that they or a loved one might get AIDS.

● Calm your child's fears. Tell your child that very few young children get AIDS. Less than 2 per cent of all AIDS cases reported by the Centers for Disease Control and Prevention occurred in children under the age of thirteen. Children shouldn't worry about catching AIDS. This is also a good time to talk to your child about having compassion for people with AIDS.

Getting it Straight:

What is AIDS?

AIDS is an acronym—a word that is made up from the first letters of other words—for:

Acquired — Something a person gets from the environment rather than heredity.

Immune — Safe, or protected. If you are immune to a disease, you are protected against it.

Deficiency — A lack or shortage of something. People with AIDS lack immunity from infections and diseases. Their bodies cannot protect them from diseases.

Syndrome — A group of symptoms or problems indicating the presence of a disease.

What Causes AIDS?

The virus that causes AIDS is known as Human Immunodeficiency Virus (HIV). The HIV virus attacks the immune system. The body becomes weak and is unable to fight off infections. People with AIDS eventually die from infections or cancers that develop because their bodies are unable to fight the infections and the weakened cells.

Myths About AIDS

There are many myths surrounding HIV/AIDS. You cannot catch HIV/AIDS by touching or hugging someone with AIDS. You cannot get HIV/AIDS from a toilet seat, a drinking fountain, or swimming pool. AIDS is not an airborne disease. This means that the germs which cause AIDS are not in the air.

How Do People Get AIDS?

People usually contract AIDS in the following ways:

● Blood transfusions are virtually safe at this time, although in the past some people obtained blood transfusions contaminated with the HIV virus.

● From sharing drug equipment or devices used by a person infected with the HIV virus.

● From having sex with someone who is infected with HIV.

● From a mother infected with the HIV virus passing the disease to a baby, during pregnancy, at birth, or by feeding the baby with breast milk.

Approximately 99.5 percent of HIV infection occurs through sexual intercourse, shared needles, or transmission from mother to fetus, according to the Harvard Medical School *Harvard Health Letter*.

Is there a cure for AIDS?

At this time there is no cure for AIDS. Experts from the National Health Institute (NHI) say that despite extensive research, no AIDS vaccine is expected in the near future. The best defense against this disease is education and prevention.

Coping With AIDS

Every family is different and there is no "right" way to cope with AIDS, says Dr. Marshall Forstein, Director of HIV Mental Health Services at Cambridge Hospital in Boston and instructor in psychiatry at Harvard Medical School. He notes:

"Families who appear to manage best are those who acknowledge the illness and discuss it directly; seek help for themselves; work through their guilt; reach a spiritual acceptance of AIDS without seeing it as a moral issue; don't blame the patient; support each other in difficult times; and respond to the person with AIDS with love and acceptance, rather than fear or judgement."

Excerpted from the April, 1994 issue of the *Harvard Health Letter* © 1994, President and Fellows of Harvard College. With permission.

Another Look:

Have you been able to calm your child's fears or dispel curiosity about HIV/AIDS with factual information? If not, use some of the excellent materials suggested under *Information Station*.

Information Station:

A host of good books have been written to help parents talk to their children about AIDS. Here are some books that you might find helpful:

AIDS Questions & Answers for Kids, Linda Schwartz, (The Learning Works, Inc., P.O. Box 6187, Santa Barbara, California 93160, 1987, revised 1993; $3.95). Factual information about AIDS. Written specifically for children in grades 5 and 6. However, you may want to have this easy-to-understand booklet as a resource in your home.

The Caregiver's Companion, Sigrid Burton, (P.O. Box 276, Canal Station, New York, NY 10013; (212) 226-0169, $10.00 plus $2.90 postage and handling). A booklet with practical information for caregivers of people with AIDS,

Children and the AIDS Virus, Rosemarie Hausherr, (Association for Care of Children's Health, 7910 Woodmont Avenue, Suite 300, Bethesda, MD 20814; (301) 654-6549, 1989, $18.00). For children to read alone or with an adult. This reassuring and open book will help children understand HIV infection and inspire them to treat people with AIDS with compassion and concern. Through photographs, straight forward text, and accounts of two children with AIDS, readers will learn about the immune system and how it fights common viruses, and about HIV and how it is and is not spread. Text in smaller type provides more detailed information for older children and adults.

Come Sit By Me, M. Merrifield, H. Collins (Association for the Care of Children's Health, 7910 Woodmont Avenue, Suite 300, Bethesda, MD 20814; (301) 654-6549; 1990, $6.95). Beautifully illustrated book about HIV infection, for preschool-age children, their families, teachers, and care providers. Includes separate information section for older students and adults.

Does AIDS Hurt?: Educating Young Children About AIDS, Marcia Quackenbush and Sylvia Villarreal, (Network Publications, a division of ETR Associates, Santa Cruz, CA, 1988; $14.95). A very helpful book for parents and teachers of children under 10. Frank, to the point, sensitive. Suggests steps for answering children's questions. Highly recommended.

The Healthy Heart: A Memoir of When Our Son Came Out, Robb Forman Dew (Addison-Wesley, 1994, $22.00) Robb Forman Dew takes the reader on a journey of acceptance as she deals with the fact that her son is gay. She helps readers understand how her family arrived at an understanding of their son far beyond tolerance. Her writing is eloquent, inspiring, and absorbing. The strength, support, and love found in Dew's family are themes that are important to all parents.

Information Station: (continued)

How Can I Tell You?: Secrecy and Disclosure with Children when a Family Member has AIDS, Mary Tasker (Association for the Care of Children's Health, 7910 Woodmont Ave., Suite 300, Bethesda, MD 20814; (301) 654-6549; 1992, $12.50). Mary Tasker, a social worker, writes that parents know their children best, and "that it is their wisdom and knowledge that should guide professional practice." Written for both parents and professionals, the book helps explore the issues that surround the disclosure of the HIV diagnosis to children. A helpful, sensitive, beautifully written book. List of books to use with children.

Kids Making Quilts for Kids, ABC Quilts Staff (Quilt Digest Press, 1992, $9.95). ABC Quilts is dedicated to making quilts for children who are born HIV-positive or addicted to drugs. Volunteers have stitched more than 142,000 quilts. The book instructs children on quilting and educates them about AIDS and drug abuse. For more information call (603) 942-9211.

Losing Uncle Tim, Mary Kate Jordan, (Albert Whitman & Company, 5747 West Howard St., Niles, Illinois 60648, 1989; $5.95). Fictional story of a young boy whose favorite uncle dies of AIDS. A warm, sensitive book about relating to people with AIDS.

Talking With Kids About AIDS, Jennifer Tiffany, Donald Tobias, and others (Cornell University Resource Center, 7 Business and Technical Park, Ithaca, NY 14850; (607) 255-1942; 1991; $9.50). Resource manual with step-by-step illustrated explanations of what HIV/AIDS is, myths, facts, and prevention. Sensitive straight talk, plus age-appropriate sample conversations for families.

The National AIDS Hotline provides referrals to local AIDS organizations as well as general information and education.
   Call 1-800-342-AIDS, 24 hours;
   1-800-344-7432, Spanish;
   1-800-243-7889, TDD, TTY.

State of Michigan Hotline:
   1-800-872-AIDS.

Parents, Families, and Friends of Lesbians and Gays (PFLAG) provides nationwide support services for families and caregivers of all people with AIDS, gay or straight. Callers will be referred to volunteers in their area. Call (202) 638-4200, Monday-Friday, 9:00 a.m. to 5:00 p.m.

Good for You!

The Code Word:
Too Smart for Strangers

At School:

Preschool health classes teach your child about strangers. Children are taught how a code word helps them to know who is a stranger. Anyone who doesn't know the code word is automatically a stranger. A code word keeps kids from having to make a judgment that they are too young to make. We suggest that children select a code word that is only known by their parents or other people who might pick them up from places like school, the bus stop, or the baby-sitter's house. Good code words are familiar to the child but not commonly used around others in public. Examples include a parent's maiden name, a nickname for the family pet, your child's favorite cookie, or the name of a favorite doll or stuffed animal. Your child should not go with anyone who doesn't know the code word.

At Home:

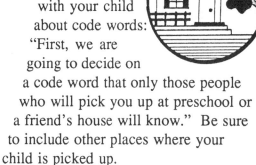

Here is an example of how to begin talking with your child about code words: "First, we are going to decide on a code word that only those people who will pick you up at preschool or a friend's house will know." Be sure to include other places where your child is picked up.

Spend a good deal of time with your child deciding about a code word. An easily remembered word is best. Be sure to practice the code word. Write the word and trace the letters with the child's fingers. This is a serious project. Your child must understand that the code word cannot be shared with others.

At Home: (continued)

Help your child remember the code word by discussing why you chose the word. Tell your child that the word is to be shared with no one except people who do the pick-ups. Say, "I will talk to those who pick you up about the code word."

Next say, "Help me remember exactly who picks you up at preschool or other places on a regular basis." Then, together name the people who will know the code word. Practice and practice who these people are.

Next Steps:

1) Teach your child what to say if someone who does not know the code word tries to pick him or her up.

2) The child should say, "I cannot go with you." Then get away from the person and tell an adult what has happened. Practice the words your child should use.

3) Practice what your child must do if a stranger tries to pick him or her up.

Getting It Straight:

Young children are often unable to tell who is a stranger and who is not. A stranger may not fit your image of a seedy man in a trenchcoat. In fact, a stranger can be a familiar face kids see everyday, such as a person who lives down the street. It's important to teach kids that a stranger is a person they do not know, and that you do not know. A stranger has never been to your house and the family doesn't know where that person lives.

The world is not filled only with strangers. It's important not to scare kids. The Child Abuse and Neglect Council of Oakland County Michigan recommends telling children that the majority of grownups never hurt kids, and most adults want to protect kids from harm.

Sergeant John Terry, Michigan State Police, Mt. Pleasant post, tells his own two kids—and those he comes in contact with on the job—that there are a lot of good people out there, but there are also some bad.

"If someone you don't know approaches you and makes you feel uncomfortable that's probably a good indicator that they're up to no good," says Terry. "Never go anywhere with a stranger, or at least don't go willingly. Scream, kick and fight. Don't give in and don't give up."

In his book, *Touchpoints: Your Child's Emotional and Behavioral Development*, child development expert T. Berry Brazelton, M.D., says that kids certainly need to be wary of strangers at school or on playgrounds who make them uncomfortable. However, wariness needs to be balanced with a sense that there are people to love and trust wholeheartedly.

Another Look:

Does your child know the code word? Does your child know who should know the code word? Does your child know when the code word should be used? Ask your child who a stranger is. Can your child give examples of someone who is a stranger and someone who is not?

Information Station:

For Children:
Ask your librarian for recommended books for pre-schoolers on the subject of strangers. Be sure to read the book alone first and think about whether your child will be helped or simply be alarmed. Here are some suggestions:

Stranger: Danger, Ellen Jackson (Horizon, 1991, $4.95).

The Berenstein Bears Learn About Strangers, Stan and Janice Berenstein (Random, 1985, $2.25).

Safety Zone, Linda D. Meyer (Warner Books, 1985, $3.50).

Never Say Yes to a Stranger, Susan Newman (Putnam, 1985, $6.95).

Information Station:

Adults will find more information to help teach children about strangers in the following:

Protect Our Children (The Department of the Attorney General, Executive Division, P.O. Box 30212, Lansing, MI 48909; (517)373-1110; free). Lists tips to help prevent abduction and resources to report a missing child.

It's OK to Say No coloring book (It's OK Press, 10585 N. Meridian St., Suite 220, Indianapolis, Indiana 44290; (317)844-9400 or fax (317)573-2299; $1.95).

Parent's Book of Child Safety, David Laskin (Ballantine Books, 1991, $4.99). Includes essentials of child safety, such as preparing your child for safe travel to school, avoiding child sexual abuse, help for latchkey children. Offers detailed advice on teaching children at each stage of development the habits and attitudes they need to keep safe. Especially good section on street smarts about strangers.

Good for You!

Sexual Abuse

At School:

Children in preschool may discuss sensitive topics in health classes. The children and their teacher discuss how to know what is a good touch and what is a bad touch. Children learn that each person has a body that belongs to them alone. They also learn that each part of the body has a name. The naming of the body parts is important so that children can tell adults if someone has touched them in a way that made them feel uncomfortable.

Your preschooler will be taught that most of the time adults touch them because they like the child and want the child to feel good. Children are also taught that sometimes touches feel bad. These bad touches may hurt or make a child feel confused or uncomfortable.

Children are told in class that there are adults who try to trick children into touching the bodies of adults and letting adults touch them. The teacher tells children that such people are lying when they say that this kind of behavior is ok.

At School: (continued)

Children are also taught that such adults may pretend to know the child or their parents, which would seem to make the offense all right. Children also learn that such people may promise treats, presents, or rides.

Your school may have a policy about which parts of the body to name and to teach your child. Please talk to your child's preschool teacher about this. You may wish to serve on a preschool committee to decide about whether to use names for body parts such as penis, anus, nipple, vulva, and vagina.

At Home:

Playing the "What If" Game

A "What If" game is very effective for teaching children how to avoid sexual abuse. This give-and-take game allows children to work on their own answers and come up with solutions. However, answers should be: **Say no, get away, tell someone.**

The game needs to zero in on a situation—not on a specific person. It is impossible to anticipate who might abuse a child. The situations should not be too specific, so children aren't frightened and so unimportant details don't confuse the real issue.

Practice the scenes several times in a non-threatening way. Repeat the "What If" game frequently as your children grow to reinforce the safety message.

There are four separate levels to the "What If" game:

1. STRANGERS: The child has no previous relationship with the person.

Example: "What if you were walking home and a person started talking to you and you felt uncomfortable. What would you do?"

2. ACQUAINTANCES: Neighbors, parents of friends, bus drivers.

Example: "What if a neighbor told you that he would give you a treat if you would go with him into his basement? What would you say?"

3. CAREGIVERS: Teachers, babysitters, relatives, close friends, youth leaders. These people have considerable influence because you have turned the child over to them for care.

Example: "What if the babysitter said you could stay up to watch a special movie if you let him or her touch you in a way you didn't like? What would you say?"

4. PEOPLE THE CHILD LOVES: Relatives, parents, or very close friends.

Example: "What if someone you loved took you for a ride and wanted to put his or her hands on you in a way that made you feel uncomfortable? What would you do?"

If you can resist the urge to answer the "What If" questions first, you will discover how your children think, what their concerns are, how they solve problems, how they think the world works, and what they know and don't know about keeping themselves safe.

The "What If" game is courtesy of Sherryll Kraizer. Ms. Kraizer has taught more than one million children through The Safe Child program.

Getting it Straight:

There is no need to go into detailed descriptions of sexual activity when talking about sexual abuse with your children. "Don't let anyone touch you on parts of your body covered by your bathing suit" covers almost all possible situations. "Don't let anyone suggest you undress" is another good rule.

It is not necessary for you to frighten the children you love and protect, but keep in mind that sexual abuse often occurs between your child and some one you all know well—a trusted community leader, a friend of the family, or a family member. It is important to know that fact and be alert to nonverbal messages of abuse from your child.

Tell your child:

- **It makes no difference who does the asking, the answer is *no*.**

- **Be firm when you say *no* and look the person in the eye.**

- **Get away from situations that make you feel uncomfortable.**

- **No one has the right to ask you to keep bad secrets. You will not be tattling if you talk to another adult.**

- **It is never your fault if someone touches you in a bad way.**

- **Even if there are bribes, threats, or physical force, come to me or another adult immediately.**

Note: If you are seeking a common sense guide to responding to your child's sexuality, try *Straight Talk: Sexuality Education for Parents and Kids 4-7*, Marilyn Ratner and Susan Chamlin for Planned Parenthood of Westchester, Inc. (Penguin Books, 1987, $4.95). Excellent material and references for both parents and children.

Another Look:

Does your child know the rules about what to do to avoid sexual abuse? Be sure your child can repeat this rule easily: "I will say no, get away, and tell someone about situations that bother me."

Information Station:

In all states, report abuse to police or Department of Protective Services or the Department of Social Services. Look in the phone book. If you have trouble finding an agency call Child Help's national 24-hour hotline (800) 4-A-CHILD; (800) 422-4453. Sexual abuse is illegal and these agencies will do an investigation.

For reporting child abuse in Michigan: Child Protective Services, a division of Michigan Department of Social Services (Look in the phone book under Michigan State Government).

Basic Facts About Child Sexual Abuse (National Committee for Prevention of Child Abuse (NCPCA), P.O. Box 94283, Chicago, IL 60690; 312-663-3520; Order Product No. 248, $4.75). Answers basic questions about abuse; discusses symptoms and contributing factors. NCPCA also publishes a free catalog listing other booklets and brochures on this topic.

Help Prevent Child Abuse and Neglect, State Bar of Michigan, Young Lawyers Section (306 Townsend Street, Lansing, MI 48933-2083; 1994; free.) Call John Gillooly at (313) 446-5501 for additional information or to obtain pamphlets. Explains Michigan Child Protection Act (Act No. 238, Public Acts of 1975). Urges everyone to help "combat this devastating problem." Excellent.

For Children:

When I Was Little Like You, Jane Porett (Child Welfare League of America, 400 First St., NW, Washington, DC, 20001; 1993; $12.95). The author tells young children how to recognize sexual abuse and to know what to do if it happens to them. Beautiful.

No No and the Secret Touch, S. Patterson and J. Feldman (National Self Esteem Resources Development Center, 176 Corte Anita, Greenbrae, CA 94904; 415-461-3401; 1993; $14.95). Package includes animal story suitable for young children; parent/teacher guides; audio tape. "Use this story to give your child lessons about your love and your willingness to listen." Especially valuable.

Good for You!

Safe Kids Are No Accident

At School:

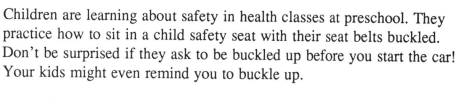

Children are learning about safety in health classes at preschool. They practice how to sit in a child safety seat with their seat belts buckled. Don't be surprised if they ask to be buckled up before you start the car! Your kids might even remind you to buckle up.

Children also learn how important it is to know their own address and telephone number. The teacher will remind students that this information is not to be shared with strangers. Children practice writing their address on a drawing of a mailbox and writing their telephone numbers on a drawing of a phone.

The teacher talks to children about how important the head is for seeing, thinking, smelling, tasting, and hearing. Children are reminded to protect their head from injury by wearing a helmet. When they ride wheeled toys children practice putting on and taking off their helmets.

At Home:

Crash Protection for Young Bodies

The body of a child is different from an adult's body. The skull is softer and more fragile. The head is heavier and much larger in proportion to the rest of the body. The rib cage is thinner and more elastic. The young child's abdomen provides only limited protection to the large internal organs. Unlike an adult, a child has a pelvis with broad gentle contours. The prominent crests which can provide an anchor point and contact area for a lap safety belt do not develop until approximately age 10; and most young children are not tall enough to use a shoulder belt. All these factors make it important to provide special crash protection for the infant and young child. Here are some guidelines for proper use of child safety seats:

- Child safety seats for infants should always face the rear of the car. This allows the back of the baby to absorb the force of the crash.

- Safety belts should be correctly routed on safety seats.

- Your child should be fastened tightly into the safety seat. Use the locking clips. Use the infant seat until your child weighs 20 pounds.

- Be sure to secure the safety seat with the vehicle's regular safety belt. The safety seat must be secured with the seat belt to keep the safety seat from being thrown around in a crash.

Air Bags

Air bags in newer cars make it all the more important that children are seated properly. The middle of the rear passenger seat is the safest position for all child safety seats because it is farthest from the most likely point of crash impact.

A child safety seat for infants must not be used in the front passenger seat when the car has an air bag on the passenger side.

While on Wheels

Pat Vranesich, R.N. is the nurse educator for community education at Children's Hospital of Michigan. She says, "it's recommended that both younger children and adults wear a helmet and preferably a helmet and pads when biking. It helps to practice what you preach and wear a helmet yourself." Wear helmets approved by the American National Standards Institute (ANSI), the Snell Memorial Foundation, or the American Society for Testing and Materials (ASTM).

At Home: (continued)

Practicing the Numbers

Quiz your child about the family phone number and address. Here is a game to help your child remember this important information.

1) Fold a 8 1/2" x 11" sheet of paper into a tiny book. Three folds will give you a 2 3/4" x 4 1/4" book.

2) If you have a stapler, staple the book near the spine (if you don't have a stapler, the three folds will still give the look of a book).

3) Label the outside of the book with your child's name and special numbers.

4) Help your child print your house number and street on the left page of the book. Have your child draw a house.

5) On the right side of the book help your child write the family's phone number. Have your child draw a phone.

6) Practice with your child until he or she is clear about these numbers.

This little book should not leave your home. Your child needs to know the numbers by heart.

The Department of Transportation estimates that survival rates in serious accidents increase by 70 percent when a child safety seat is properly used.

Getting it Straight:

All 50 states now have child passenger safety laws. The child restraint law in Michigan (Public Act 117 of 1981) says:

Children under one year of age must be properly buckled into a child safety seat *regardless of where they ride in the vehicle.* Children at least one-year-old (but less than four) must also be in a child safety seat if they ride in the front seat. All children in Michigan between the ages of 4 and 16 must wear safety belts when seated in either the front or the back seat. (House Bill 4220; 1990 addendum to Public Act 117.)

Check the manual that comes with your child safety seat. Find out from the manual the maximum weight and height limits of the safety seat. When a child reaches the maximum weight of and/or height for a toddler car seat, a booster seat may be used. The booster seat helps you put your pre-schooler at a level so you can fasten your child in with the seat belt found in your vehicle. Read the manufacturer's directions carefully to ensure you are using the child safety seat correctly.

Bikes

Cyclists ages 14 and under are at five times greater risk for injury than are older cyclists. Head injury is the leading cause of death in bicycle crashes for all age groups. Properly worn bicycle helmets have been shown to reduce the risk of head injury by 85 percent and the risk of brain injury by almost 90 percent.

Getting it Straight:

Many experts do not recommend that parents carry babies or toddlers on their bicycles, due to increased risk of injury to the child. If you're a bike-riding parent with a rear-mounted bike seat, remember to use the harness straps to secure children over the age of one. Any child riding in a bicycle trailer also needs to be strapped in. Children must wear toddler-sized helmets that meet the safety standards. Parents need to wear a helmet, too. (See While on Wheels, page 62.)

Bike Helmets

Riders of all ages should look for a helmet with a stiff, smooth outer shell to lessen the impact of a fall and protect against sharp objects. Be sure the helmet has an energy-absorbing liner to absorb the impact of a fall and a chin strap and fastener to keep the helmet from shifting or falling off in an accident. You'll find these features in a helmet bearing the seal of approval from the **American National Standards Institute (ANSI),** the **Snell Memorial Foundation,** or the **American Society for Testing and Materials (ASTM).** Please look for helmets with these seals at your local bike store or large retailer such as Meijers, Sears, K-Mart or WalMart.

Information Station:

Bicycle Safety Camp (video), The Injury Prevention Program of the American Academy of Pediatrics produced by Broadstreet Productions (AAP Publications, P.O. Box 927, Elk Grove Village, IL 60009-0927; 1989; $9.95 plus $4.50 shipping). Twenty-five minute video for parents and kids ages 5-9. All the important lessons on bike safety are illustrated.

Emergency Medical Treatment and Infants; Emergency Medical Treatment: Children. Both published in cooperation with National Safety Council. Also available in Spanish (EMT Inc., P.O. Box 938, Wilmette, IL 60091; 708-251-5215; $8.95 each).

Getting the Right Safety Seat for Your Child, Michigan Office of Highway Safety Planning (300 S. Washington Square, Suite 300, Lansing, MI 48913; 517-334-5200; 1993; free). Excellent. Call 517-334-5200 to locate the child safety seat rental programs in your county.

Another Look:

✓ Do all family members buckle up?

✓ Are family members wearing helmets when they bike, rollerblade, and skateboard?

✓ Does your preschooler know his or her telephone number and address?

Information Station:

A Parent's Guide to Child Safety, Laura Coyne, editor (National Safety Council, 1121 Spring Lake Drive, Itasca, IL 60143-3201; 1-800-621-7619; $5.00—you can call and place your order on Visa or Mastercard).

Fifty Ways to Keep Your Child Safe, Susan K. Golant (Lowell House, 1992, $10.95). From fire protection to AIDS prevention to sexual abuse, this book gives you a positive approach to keeping your child safe.

Safe At School: Awareness and Action for Parents of Kids Grades K-12, Carol Silverman Saunders (Free Spirit, 1994, $14.95). This is a good general book that is also applicable to pre-K parents. Covers how to form a parent safety group, how to work with administrators on all aspects of school safety, including fire safety and sexual abuse.

Sudden Impact: An Occupant Protection Fact Book (DOT HS 807 743), Office of Occupant Protection NTS-10, U.S. Department of Transportation, National Highway Traffic Safety Administration, (400 Seventh Street S.W., NTS-13, Washington, DC 20590). One copy free. Outstanding. Well written. Vital information on car safety for all family members.

1993 Shopping Guide to Child Safety Seats, developed by the American Academy of Pediatrics. From the Michigan Department of State Police, Office of Highway Safety Planning, (300 S. Washington Square, Suite 300, Knapps Center, Lansing, MI 48913 or call 517-334-5200). Up-to-date information on manufacturer, type, safety features, and price range. All products listed meet Federal Motor Vehicle Safety Standards 213.

To receive a brochure on bike helmets, send a self-addressed, stamped envelope to the American Academy of Pediatrics, The Injury Prevention Program (TIPP), 141 Northwest Point Blvd., P.O. Box 927, Elk Grove Village, IL 60009.

Recalls on Child Safety Seats

When you purchase a child safety seat it is very important to mail in the registration card that comes with the seat. When you return the registration card to the manufacturer, the manufacturer can then contact you **directly** if there is a need to recall the seat you have purchased. You want to hear from the manufacturer if there is something wrong with the seat you own. Take five minutes and send the safety seat registration card to the manufacturer. Your child's safety depends on you.

The Auto Safety Hotline has up-to-date information about child safety seat recalls. Call them at 1-800-424-9393.

Good for You!

Bang! Bang! You're Dead!

At School:

Violence on television is a public health problem. According to University of Michigan professors Leonard Eron and L. Rowell Huesmann, TV violence is every bit as dangerous to kids as smoking or drinking.

The amount of violence that children watch on television is strongly related to aggressive behavior in later years. Professors Eron and Huesmann interviewed almost two thousand children in five countries. The children who watched more violence on TV were more aggressive, regardless of country.

Television is not the single cause of all violent behavior. However, professor Eron estimates that television is responsible for approximately 10 percent of the violent behavior in the country. He states: "If we could reduce violence by 10 percent, that would be a great achievement."

One part of the solution to a problem of violence lies in teaching preschool children how to handle aggression. In preschool health classes children are taught ways to solve problems peacefully and to avoid conflicts. They may use puppets and play things to work on problem solving.

At School: (continued)

When quarreling occurs, children may be asked to tell what happened. The teacher asks that while one child talks, the other stays quiet. The teacher may ask for corrections in the story before calling on the other child to tell her or his side of the dispute. Children are asked to talk about how the events made them feel and how they think the other child feels. They are also asked to decide how they would like the other child to behave, and what they will do differently. The teacher and the children talk about what each child could do differently next time.

At Home:

TV Violence: What Messages Are Your Kids Learning?

Sesame Street or Ninja Turtles?

The power of television to influence attitudes and behaviors is tremendous. Most homes in America have at least one television. Fifty percent of the children in this country between the ages of 6 and 17 have their own bedroom television sets! The average child watches 4 to 5 hours of television per day. Most children spend more time watching television than interacting with adults. The television programs that your child is exposed to help to shape his or her view of the world.

TV violence has a greater effect on children than adults. Professor Eron's findings show that what you watch as an adult won't have nearly the effect of what you saw when you were eight or younger. This is because young children do not always understand the differences between fiction and reality. Children often think that life on TV is reality.

Some young children have imitated behaviors seen on television with tragic results. One five-year-old boy lit a fire after watching a popular cartoon show that resulted in the death of his two-year-old sister. Other examples of such behavior are common today.

Kids are bombarded with violence in their favorite action hero cartoons. The late Professor John Condry at Cornell University found that typical action/adventure cartoons contain an average of 25 acts of violence per hour.

At Home: (continued)

The message that kids get from these shows is that the way to get what you want is through the use of force or power.

Parents can take steps to counter the negative messages seen on television. Here are some things that you can do:

- Limit the amount of time your child spends watching television to 1 to 2 hours per day.
- Monitor the programs that your child watches.
  Turn off objectionable programs.
- Discuss programs with your child. How do the TV messages relate to your family's values?
- Encourage your child to watch programs in which characters help and care for each other. These programs do have positive influences.
- Use TV as an educational tool. Watch educational programs with your child.
- Talk about the programs after you watch.

What are some alternatives to watching television?

1) Write a story. Have your child tell you what to write. Then help your child draw or cut out pictures to illustrate the story.
2) Play games like Go Fish or Candyland.
3) Play in a sandbox together.
4) Go for a walk in the park.
5) Read, read, read. Talk about what you have read.
6) Listen to the radio.
7) Listen to stories and plays on cassettes.
8) Ride bikes and tricycles together. Be sure to wear helmets.

9) Cut out pictures and make a scrap book about your child's favorite subject.
10) Visit the library. Attend a story hour.
11) Cut out pictures from old magazines to teach geometric shapes.
12) Arrange to have another child visit.
13) Go to the zoo.
14) String a set of beads.
15) Write a letter together to a relative.
16) Let your child wash dishes in the sink.
17) Teach your child to set the table. Count the forks, spoons, and knives.
18) Make bread, muffins, cookies, or cake together. Talk about measuring the ingredients and mixing the dough.
19) Make a batch of homemade clay. See *Information Station* for recipe. Create clay objects together.
20) Finger paint. See *Information Station* for recipe.
21) Set up a play corner with a large cardboard box filled with dress-up clothes, blankets, and any extra household items (plastic dishes, pots, pans, dolls, or teddy bears).

Getting it Straight:

TV violence is recognized by experts and government officials as having a negative influence on the behavior of young people. Television and movies saturate young peoples' lives with aggression. Attorney General Janet Reno stated: "Too often America has become numbed to violence because it has just been drowned in it, day in and day out."

Attorney General Reno challenged the television industry to take measures to voluntarily reduce the amount of violence in programs or face government regulation. Contact your local station about programs that you believe are unacceptable. Five letters from parents can make a difference! See *Another Look* for national contacts.

Most television programs are written to attract ratings and do not have the best interest of children in mind. The following programs are recommended for children ages 2 through 5. (This list is not meant to be exhaustive; there may be many other good shows as well):

- *Mr. Roger's Neighborhood*
- *Sharon, Lois & Bram's Elephant Show*
- *Zoobilee*
- *Polka Dot Door*
- *Reading Rainbow*
- *Shining Time Station*
- *Sesame Street*
- *Barney and Friends*
- *Lamb Chop's Play-Along*

Another Look:

One of the dangers of watching too much television, even educational programs, is that children do not spend enough time interacting with others, playing, and exercising. Have you tried any of the activities listed under the *At Home* section?

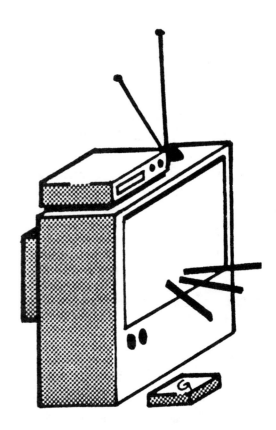

National contacts to commend TV programs, or complain about their content.

ABC: Audience Information, 77 W. 66th St., New York, NY 10023

CBS: Audience Services, 51 W. 52 St., New York, NY 10019

NBC: Children's Programming, 3000 W. Alameda Ave., Room 246, Burbank, CA 91523

Information Station:

Modeling Dough Recipes:

Uncooked Modeling Dough

Ingredients:
4 cups flour	Food coloring
2 cups salt	Water

Procedure:
Slowly add enough water to the flour and salt to make a soft, workable dough. Stop when the dough is still a little dry. Add food coloring. Work by hand for 10 minutes.

Stove-top Modeling Dough

Ingredients:
1 cup flour	2 tsps. cream of
1/2 cup salt	tartar
2 T. cooking oil	1 cup water
	Food coloring

Procedure:
Stir mixture over low heat until it begins to pull away from the sides of the pan. Remove from pan and knead until smooth. Keep refrigerated in an airtight container.

Finger Paint Recipe:

Finger Paint

Ingredients:
   1/4 cup cornstarch
   2 cups cold water
   Food coloring

Procedure:
Mix cornstarch with cold water. Boil until the mixture thickens. Cool and pour into containers, such as baby food jars. Add food coloring; stir and cover. Makes three jars. After the first use, stir to regain the original consistency.

Children need finger paint paper, clothes which can be washed, and water for hand washing for a finger painting project. In the summer, a picnic table outdoors is a good spot for this activity.

What Should I Tell the Kids?, Ava L. Siegler, Ph.D. (Penguin Books USA Inc., 375 Hudson St., New York, NY 10014, 1993, $21.00). Good section on television and violence.

Making Things: The Handbook of Creative Discovery, Ann Wiseman (Little Brown, 1973, $14.95).

The Muppets Make Puppets, Cheryl Henson (Workman, 1994, $16.95).

365 Days of Creative Play, Sheila Ellison and Judity Gray (Forward March Press, 1991, $14.95).

Good for You!

Avoiding Danger: Household Poisons

At School:

Health classes at school are helping children become more aware of the dangers of poisons. For example, the teacher may prepare a box of cans and bottles which have poison labels. The box will be marked UNSAFE. The teacher will encourage children to talk about products with the POISON word or symbol and discuss how poisonous substances make children sick. Your child may be alerted to the fact that even small amounts of alcohol can be poisonous to children.

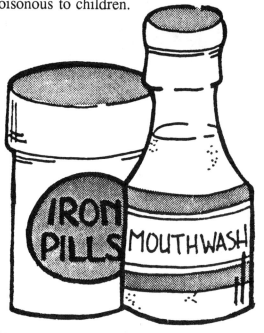

At Home:

A good rule to teach your child about poisons is:

If you aren't sure that something is safe, don't sniff, taste, swallow or play with it.

If all poisons were labeled with skull and crossbones, child proofing would be a whole lot easier. Certain items are known to be dangerous, but who would guess that a child could die from a few gulps of mouthwash or a handful of iron pills.

Iron pill overdose is the most common cause of early childhood death by poisoning, accounting for nearly one-third of all deaths each year. Some mouthwashes contain 27 percent alcohol. One ounce of mouthwash that is swallowed can be dangerous to young children. Five to nine ounces can cause the death of a young child.

A list of common household items that are potential poisons is found on the chart on page 75. Put these poisons out of the reach of young children. **Post this list so all family members can help keep children safe.**

Getting it Straight:

- Almost one million young children are poisoned or nearly poisoned each year. Families can't afford to ignore the issues of poisons in the home.

- Tossing a briefcase or purse where your child can get into it can be unwise if the purse contains medicine, cigarettes, or cosmetics.

- Poison centers say that calls come in between 5:00 p.m. and bed time, times when families are especially busy. Many kids get into trouble while adults sleep late on the weekend.

- Child-resistant tops don't mean child proof. Store medicine, household chemicals, and such items as insect repellent under lock and key.

If your child gets into poisons, remain calm, call your local poison control center, doctor, or hospital. Save the label or container of the suspected poison for identification. Be sure to have syrup of ipecac, which induces vomiting, on hand, but don't use it unless directed to do so by a poison-control expert or physician. If your child vomits, save a sample of the vomited material for analysis.

If your child has spilled a toxic substance on himself, wash the area. If a toxin has gotten into the eye, flush it with water that is room temperature. If your child becomes unconscious:

✓ Keep his airway open, and call an emergency squad.

✓ Give artificial respiration or cardio-pulmonary resuscitation (CPR) if needed.

Do not give fluids to an unconscious child. If the child is vomiting, turn the head so the material drains out. If the child is having convulsions: call an emergency squad. Do not restrain the child, but position the child away from objects that might cause injury. Loosen clothing at neck and waist. Give artificial respiration (CPR), if needed.

In Michigan call, **1-800-POISON-1**. That's **1-800-764-7661**. Callers in southeastern Michigan will automatically reach Children's Hospital, Detroit; those in western Michigan and the Upper Peninsula will reach Blodgett Hospital, Grand Rapids. The service operates 24 hours a day. **Other states call 911 for information.**

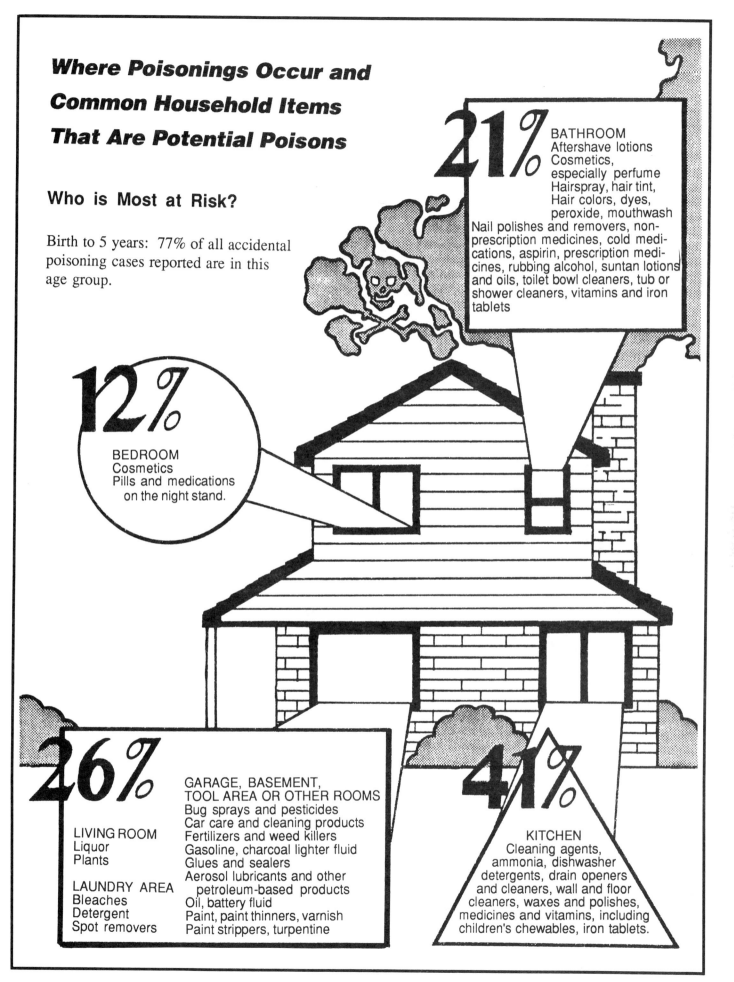

Where Poisonings Occur and Common Household Items That Are Potential Poisons

Who is Most at Risk?

Birth to 5 years: 77% of all accidental poisoning cases reported are in this age group.

21%
BATHROOM
Aftershave lotions
Cosmetics, especially perfume
Hairspray, hair tint, Hair colors, dyes, peroxide, mouthwash
Nail polishes and removers, nonprescription medicines, cold medications, aspirin, prescription medicines, rubbing alcohol, suntan lotions and oils, toilet bowl cleaners, tub or shower cleaners, vitamins and iron tablets

12%
BEDROOM
Cosmetics
Pills and medications on the night stand.

26%
LIVING ROOM
Liquor
Plants

LAUNDRY AREA
Bleaches
Detergent
Spot removers

GARAGE, BASEMENT, TOOL AREA OR OTHER ROOMS
Bug sprays and pesticides
Car care and cleaning products
Fertilizers and weed killers
Gasoline, charcoal lighter fluid
Glues and sealers
Aerosol lubricants and other petroleum-based products
Oil, battery fluid
Paint, paint thinners, varnish
Paint strippers, turpentine

41%
KITCHEN
Cleaning agents, ammonia, dishwasher detergents, drain openers and cleaners, wall and floor cleaners, waxes and polishes, medicines and vitamins, including children's chewables, iron tablets.

Help in Time of Emergency
Please Post Near Phone

Poison Control Center: In Michigan, 1-800-POISON-1.
That's 1-800-764-7661.

Callers in southeastern Michigan will automatically reach Children's Hospital; those in western Michigan and the Upper Peninsula will reach Blodgett Hospital, Grand Rapids. The service operates 24 hours a day. **Other states call 911 for information.**

(Child) _____ 's allergies are _____

(Child) _____ 's allergies are _____

(Child's name) _____ weighs _____ pounds

(Child's name) _____ weighs _____ pounds

Work numbers for family members or special people to call in case of emergency.

(Name) _____ (Telephone No.) (____) _____

(Name) _____ (Telephone No.) (____) _____

(Name) _____ (Telephone No.) (____) _____

Our physician is Dr. _____

   Office Phone _____

   Home Phone _____

Our local hospital is _____ **Phone** (____) _____

Directions to our house: (Be sure to write your address and directions below.)

Address: _____ Telephone No. (____) _____

_____

Directions: _____

_____

_____

(example) "Our address is 1623 West Belmont, Pontiac. Our street is west of Woodward Ave. If you are heading north on Woodward, turn left (use the turnaround) on to Diversey Road and head west about 1/2 mile. Our street is the fifth cross street off Diversey Road. Turn left onto Belmont. We are the third house on the left. Our house is blue with yellow shutters. I've put the outside lights on."

Call 911 in any emergency.
They'll contact the Police and Fire Department.

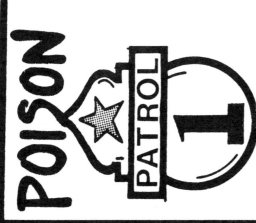

Poison Control Certificate

POISON PATROL 1

This certifies that

_____

*knows the rule for poisons and
the signs that warn of poisonous products.*

_____
signed

Rule for Poison Safety
If you aren't sure something is safe,
don't sniff, taste, swallow, or play with it.

UNSAFE

You and your preschool child can search the kitchen, where over 40 percent of poisonings occur. After your search fill in the attached Poison Control Certificate. Post the certificate in a prominent place to remind all of the family to beware of poisons in the home.

The Author

Dr. Alice R. McCarthy is a nationally known civic leader, educator, and writer. Dr. McCarthy is a Cornell University graduate in early childhood development and education. She completed her doctorate at Wayne State University in 1986. Her work concerned human growth over the life span and curriculum development. Since her degree work, Dr. McCarthy has devoted her energies to substance abuse prevention, family education, and research. She writes and edits a variety of materials to help parents understand current issues affecting the family.

Between 1987 and 1994, Dr. McCarthy prepared a column—*The Advisory Board*— for the Parent Talk Page of the *Detroit Free Press*. In 1994 she is preparing two columns for the Suburban Communications Corporation. One column, *All About Families*, features professionals who answer family questions. The other column, *Generation to Generation*, offers advice to grandparents. Dr. McCarthy has been the executive editor of a number of manuals and magazines for families related to child development, family issues, and health.

In 1991 and 1992 Dr. McCarthy was the executive editor of **Good For You!,** a 48-page, four-color health information magazine developed with a federal grant designed to expand family involvement in the *Michigan Model for Comprehensive School Health Education*. In 1993, her company, Bridge Communications, Inc., published a four-color magazine entitled **Healthy Families: Healthy Children** for *Growing Healthy*, a national health education program taught in Oakland County. These magazines reached nearly one million parents in Michigan and across the United States.

Currently Dr. McCarthy is involved in several research projects related to families and health, including a grant-funded initiative to write and publish a family and health curriculum.

Since 1992, Dr. McCarthy's company has been publishing four-page health newsletters for families with children in grades K-3, 4-5, and 6-8. The four-color newsletters are published twice yearly and purchased for distribution. Over one million newsletters reached families between 1993 and 1994. The newsletters are now being distributed nationally.

Dr. McCarthy began her advocacy for health education over twenty years ago by initiating a health education curriculum in the school system her five children attended.

Dr. McCarthy's civic roles are extensive. She is the past chairperson of the Board of Regents of Lake Superior State University and is currently chairperson of the Board of Directors of the Merrill-Palmer Institute, Wayne State University. Her achievements have been honored nationally and state-wide with awards and commendations.

ORDER FORM

Healthy Preschoolers: At School and At Home

Please mail or fax (810-644-8546) this order to **Bridge Communications, Inc., 1450 Pilgrim Rd., Birmingham, MI 48009.**

(PLEASE PRINT)

Name:_____ Title:_____

Organization/School: _____

Address:_____ Zip: _____

Phone: (   ) _____ Fax: (   ) _____

Single Copy $7.98 (in Michigan add 6% sales tax - $.48 each) plus $3.50 shipping and handling for up to three books. UPS shipping charges will be added to orders of four copies or more.

Books from Bridge Communications, Inc. are available at <u>quantity</u> discounts with bulk purchase for educational purposes (500 and over). Contact Bridge Communications, Inc. for details at (810)646-1020, or (810)646-5583, or FAX us at (810)644-8546.

1.   Number of books you wish to order? _____

2.   _____ Payment enclosed in the amount of $_____.
     Please make checks payable to Bridge Communications, Inc.

     _____ We will be mailing a purchase order.

     _____ We need an invoice for _____ books and shipping fees.

3.   Please sign here: _____

4.   Please make any comments you wish here.

_____

_____

Questions? Call (810)646-1020 <u>or</u> (810)646-5583 <u>or fax to</u>: (810)644-8546

THANK YOU FOR YOUR ORDER.